EVERYTHING

Stephanie Ehmke

What If God Wants
More Than Your Heart?

ISBN 979-8-88644-530-5 (Paperback)
ISBN 979-8-88644-532-9 (Hardcover)
ISBN 979-8-88644-531-2 (Digital)

Covenant Books
11661 Hwy 707
Murrells Inlet, SC 29576
www.covenantbooks.com

To my husband and best friend, Todd,
and our incredible children, Sydney and Cody.
You were each worth fighting for and I love you.
Thank you for trusting me with sharing our families' story so openly.

To my dear sister-in-Christ, Ida.
Thank you for paying attention to God's nudge
to remind me it was time to write this book.

To my tribe: Laura, Renae, Sydney, Dena,
Stephanie, Tara, Ida, and Susan.
Thank you for reading, encouraging, and praying me through this endeavor.
The journey has been sweeter knowing I wasn't alone on it.

Special acknowledgment to my daughter, Sydney.
I couldn't have finished this book without you.
There is nothing more humbling and holy than having you pray over me
on the many occasions when I thought I couldn't move forward.

And finally, Todd, thank you for daily living
out a story of redemption with me so others might see Jesus.

Contents

Introduction

"What does God want from me?"

These six little words have flowed through my mind off and on in various forms for the past twenty years of following Jesus. Sometimes they are inquisitive, truly wondering, "What's next?" on this journey through life. But most of the time, if I'm honest, probably 95 percent of the time, these words flow from a place of irritation and confusion. Life events have just not matched what I expected when I gave my life to Jesus. Maybe you can relate.

I'll be the first to admit that I am nowhere near perfect or the standard of holiness I see Jesus calling his followers to in Scripture, but I do try, and isn't that what counts? I've tried with all my heart and soul to live a life that honors God and follows where he leads. Still, at times, life has felt like one big never-ending assault on my soul. Don't misunderstand, I love my life, and there have been some truly beautiful seasons that I wouldn't trade for anything. I just confess that in some moments I find myself wondering, "Is it too much to ask for a little help and protection from God?" I mean, c'mon, "What does God want from me?"

The truth is, there is a crucial aspect of the Christian life that no one seems to talk much about when we are first getting to know Jesus. It is, however, one that is vitally important if we who follow him are to live the life of freedom for which he has called us. Without this knowledge, the brokenness of this life, the hatred in our world, and the assaults of the enemy will be misconstrued and we will blame God, missing out on the intimacy and connection we so vitally need to endure those hard times.

Additionally, it will be hard to keep grounded in the seasons when life is good as these are times when, in our humanness, it is so easy to forget how much we need God.

So what is it? What is this crucial aspect of the Christian life that we so desperately need to be told that no one seems to talk about when it comes to following Jesus?

He…wants…*everything*.

Yes, he wants our hearts as soon as we come to him in faith, believing in his work of salvation on our behalf, but this is only the beginning. It's what marks the start of the life-long journey God has for us to come into the fullness of who he made us to be. For those of us who choose to fully enter in, it will be the wildest adventure we could ever take, full of ups, downs, twists, and turns. We will experience the highest highs of mountaintop experiences with God and the lowest of lows in the valleys of sorrow with him. And it will be worth it, all of it, but it will cost us…everything.

In Matthew 16:24–25 (NIV), Jesus tells his disciples, *"Whoever wants to be my disciple must deny themselves and take up their cross and follow me. For whoever wants to save their life will lose it, but whoever loses their life for me will find it."*

There is so much more to these verses than a simple reading implies. It's not about denying ourselves the things we enjoy. In taking up our cross, we are taking on the mission of Christ, and choosing to deny ourselves "everything" that distracts from his purpose and glory being fulfilled in our lives. If we live solely for ourselves, our wants, needs, thoughts, desires, and purposes we may have a good life, a great life even, but lose the life God has for us to experience with him. But if we choose to surrender "everything" on the surface, losing what the world believes will bring happiness, we will truly find a life with God that exceeds all expectations.

It sounds good, doesn't it?

My guess is, at this point, some of you may be thinking, "Yes, yes, it does. This is the life with Jesus that I want. How do I get more of him?" Great! This tells me you've experienced enough of Jesus to know life with him is worth it. So keep reading because I believe there is more for you in what I have to share. For others, this may be a really difficult concept to grasp and one that's even harder to consider. You may be thinking, "Why? Why would anyone surrender everything in their lives to a God they can't even see? Isn't my faith, allegiance, and commitment to try and be a good person enough?" If your thoughts are somewhere in this camp, I understand and have been where you are in my own journey. Please, keep reading because I believe there is more here for you too.

The truth is, there is a reason why this aspect of the Christian life is not talked about much in our early days of faith. Simply put, it's not just hard to embrace the idea of surrendering everything to Jesus; it's impossible to do on our own. Early in our faith, we are not ready for such lofty notions. Surrendering our hearts was a big enough step.

Jesus is such a gentleman. He knows our human frailty and when we are ready to go deeper. When the time is right, he will begin to seek more of our trust in every area of life, but graciously, not all at once. In those seasons, he will not make us surrender that which we hold so dear. No, surrender and trust are always our choices and he will honor what we choose. Our decision will simply pull us closer to him or keep us at a distance.

Let me be clear about something, though. Jesus does not want everything from us because he is an egotistical narcissist, not by any stretch. His purposes, unlike ours, are always pure, and his only desire is to have a place in our hearts above everything, the place that only he deserves. Anything in our lives that becomes more important, an idol or something we trust in above him, he will ask for us to surrender so that we may enjoy the fullness of life with him.

Again, it is not easy, but it is worth it.

There are many who may believe as an ordained pastor and licensed professional Christian counselor that I have to take this stance. I mean, isn't that what I'm paid to do, to help people trust God more? Yes, of course, there is truth to this thought, but on the pages that follow, you will not read the words of a pastor or counselor. What you will experience, with much rawness, is my life as a woman who loves Jesus and how he has one by one asked for everything I've held dear and trusted in above him—my heart, my past, my pain, my marriage, my career, my pride, my children, my security, my aspirations, my ministry, and many, many more things. I will share honestly, the pain, the wrestling, the confusion, and the outcomes in the hope that you will find the strength to trust God in whatever season you may find yourself.

Even more so, I hope you will find on these pages that Jesus's desire for everything is bound to his heart to redeem every single part of our stories. The broken parts we choke to speak about and the beautiful parts we want to rely upon. All of it, all of who we are as individuals, Jesus wants to embrace and make pure for his glory and for our good.

Jesus has asked for everything from me and with trembling hands, clenched throat, and tear-filled eyes I have given it; quite imperfectly, but willingly. My prayer is that you may find the encouragement from my story to do so as well.

He is worth it.

Part 1

EVERYTHING BROKEN

My days have passed, my plans are shattered.

—Job 17:11 (NIV)

My sacrifice, O God, is a broken spirit;
a broken and contrite heart you,
God, will not despise.

—Psalm 51:17 (NIV)

1

Shattered

*Much-Afraid, do you love me enough to
accept the postponement and the apparent
contradiction of the promise, and to go
down there with me into the desert?*

—Hannah Hurnard,
Hinds' Feet on High Places

*It was the moment that changed everything about my faith and the way I
live, though at the time I didn't know it. There I sat, all alone in my car for
nearly two hours in the parking lot of the Burger King across the street from
my subdivision. It was a brutally cold, windy February morning in Missouri
with gusts of wind so strong they rattled my SUV. Everyone driving by
appeared to be in such a hurry to get on with the day. No one knew my
life had just been shattered. Everything I trusted had been shaken, turned
completely upside down, and yet no one even seemed to notice me slumped
over the steering wheel, crying so hard I could barely breathe. Every now and
then the tears would stop for a moment and I'd try to drink some coffee, now
lukewarm at best, but mostly I would stare out the windshield in a daze.
There was no in-between, either a torrential downpour of tears or dazed
confusion. This was how I spent the morning that forever changed the trajectory of my life and what I believed about faith, hope, and Jesus. This was the
moment when I was invited by God to begin surrendering…everything.*

3

Everything that had happened in the previous twelve hours felt like a complete contradiction of what God had been leading me to hope and believe over the past several months. Instead of being "sheltered under his wings" as the psalmist declares (Ps. 91:4 NET), I felt like I'd been punched in the gut and thrown into a ditch. I had dared to hope in Jesus for a different life, one full of joy and happiness, and instead what God seemed to allow was unimaginable pain and heartache. To say I didn't understand would be a horrendous understatement.

It had only been about a year and a half since I had completely given my heart back to Jesus. I had asked him to be my Savior at age twelve, but early on (for reasons I'll explain later) made the choice I didn't need him. However, at the age of twenty-seven, I desperately saw with absolute clarity my need for him to lead my life and surrendered my heart fully back to him, not only as my Savior but also as my Lord.

Initially, I found relief in the surrender. I had made a mess of my life to this point and no longer wanted or needed the responsibility of being in control. I was certain my newfound love and dedication to Jesus would bring the peace for which my heart ached. Turns out that was not the case as my constant companion during this season was confusion.

On the surface, my life appeared perfect. My family looked like we had achieved the much sought-after American Dream. My husband Todd and I had been high school sweethearts and were now in our seventh year of marriage with two children, a boy and a girl. We lived in a nice neighborhood on the corner lot of bustling cul-de-sac, and each drove a shiny new car. We both had great full-time jobs, extended families that loved our children and us well, yet something was terribly wrong. We had everything the world says should make us happy, but we were miserable.

Faith had not seemed to work out for me when I was younger, but even though I had walked away from God as a teenager, I had grown up in a solid, Christ-centered church and now believed (maybe out of desperation) that Jesus was the missing piece for me. I also truly believed he was the missing piece for my family as well.

The problem was, the closer I got to Jesus during that season, the worse my marriage and family became. It didn't make any sense to me.

In all fairness to my husband, prior to our marriage, there was very little about my life that would have indicated Jesus held any kind of significance to me or that I had any kind of faith. I remember giving Todd a Bible our senior year of high school and talking about matters of faith occasionally, but other than that, nothing in my life resembled a heart that was following Jesus. Absolutely nothing.

So when I now decided to shift my life back in the direction of Jesus, I moved carefully, treading lightly in those early months when I began to reengage church and matters of faith. While I was very intentional during that time about talking with Todd about my reignited faith, I was also very careful not to come across as "too religious" or make it appear like I was trying to convert him. I wanted him to figure out where Jesus fit into his life on his own. Still, an apparent hostility grew in him toward my faith, as it became more of a priority for me.

I wouldn't say I went overboard by any means. The extent of my relationship with Jesus during this time was simply Sunday morning church and reading my Bible through the week (which I only did when he wasn't home). The one time I brought the Bible to read in bed you'd have thought I put an open fire on the comforter. Something about these small steps seemed to distance Todd from me. We began fighting regularly about silly things, but more specifically, about me taking the kids to church every Sunday morning. In his eyes, since he typically worked six days a week, I was breaking up our family on the one day we could all be together. I would invite him to attend with us, but that was only met with rolled eyes and cranky words.

It was during this season of life that the events of 9-11 forever changed our world. While we were not directly affected by the events of that day, the eternal questions that so many wrestled with about where God was during such tragedies began to weigh heavily on Todd. Questions came to the surface in many of our conversations about the purpose and meaning of human life and why we are here at all. I did my best, with my limited knowledge at the time, to share what I knew, but my attempts to console him were continually met with sarcasm and rejection. One evening, after a particularly hard day of work, I remember Todd yelling through angry tears, "What is the purpose of all of this? And don't give me any of that b——— s——— about God and purpose. You live, you die, and then you're worm food."

That night crushed me as I saw the profound depths of Todd's hopelessness while feeling powerless to do anything about it.

The next few months, I would continue to see a rapid decline in our marriage and family. Daily, I was begging God to show up and reveal himself to Todd, asking for him to save our family, but no positive change came. The only noticeably consistent change during this time was that of Todd pulling slowly away from me and the kids.

He worked all the time, usually somewhere between seventy to eighty hours, six days per week. Because he was gone so much, I took on most of the daily responsibilities of running the home and taking care of our two children. The times when we did get to spend together as a family were especially tense as Todd could feel the distance between himself and the kids. They were little at the time, ages three and seven, getting up late and going to bed early, which meant Todd was usually gone before they woke and home late after they'd already gone to bed.

I witnessed the toll this was taking on our family when Todd told our son Cody, then three years old, he loved him before bed one Sunday evening as they sat on the couch together. Cody looked at him and said nothing. The protective mama bear within me sensed danger, so quickly I rose up, whisking Cody off to bed before Todd could say anything. Upon returning, Todd was in a rage, fuming, "How can my own son not tell me he loves me!"

My only response was to simply say, "Sweetie, you're never here, and he just doesn't know you." This was not the answer he wanted to hear, so he just shook his head in disbelief and walked away.

Fast on the heels of this event, Todd pulled even further away by deciding to buy an old house to remodel and flip about forty-five minutes away from our home. For the next few months, he would spend most of his time outside of work there. The endeavor was cloaked in words about investing for our future, but deep down, I knew it was just an excuse not to be with us. There were times when we as a family engaged in work on the house together, but for the most part, this was Todd's way to hide from us.

For me, the one positive thing during this season was how my heart was falling more and more in love with Jesus. Daily, I was soaking up every book, every radio show, every sermon I could get my hands on about doing life with him. My young, naive heart mused, "If I am this committed to my faith, surely my Savior won't let my family fall apart. At some point, he is going to intervene." I wasn't sure if I truly believed these thoughts or if I was just desperately trying to convince myself.

୨୦

During this time, one of the radio shows I would regularly listen to on my way to work in the mornings was *Focus on the Family*. For the most part, I always found the broadcasts helpful and encouraging, but there was one day in particular that rocked my world and messed with my brain for several weeks. I don't remember specifically the name of the woman who shared her story, but I do remember how it profoundly affected me.

The short version is this woman came to know Jesus as her Savior at eighteen years of age and, not long after, was carjacked and sexually assaulted. She shared the trauma and devastation, but also about forgiveness and love (yes, I said *love*) for her attacker. I replayed her story over and over in my head for weeks and finally came to one logical conclusion. I could never love Jesus like that, not in that way.

I struggled greatly with this thought because I knew I was basically putting up a wall in my blossoming relationship with Jesus. I was letting him know, clearly, our relationship could only go so far.

Something deep inside of me knew this was wrong thinking, but I also knew I wasn't capable of the kind of love and forgiveness the woman on the radio displayed for her attacker simply because she was a follower of Jesus.

The question lingered heavily in the air around me: "How does one build a relationship with Jesus when you're telling him you can only trust him so far?"

As things at home continued to rapidly deteriorate, this woman's story plagued my thoughts daily. How could she love Jesus that way? How could she trust him after what happened? Why would she trust him and why couldn't I just let it go? And what, if anything, did her story have to do with me and what was going on in my life?

No concrete answers came, but I soon found myself wading in Scripture, for the first time ever, into the book of Job. As I read of Job and his commitment to God in the midst of unimaginable tragedy, my mind kept wandering back to the woman on the radio. Both she and Job had fully given their hearts to God and look at what happened to them; what God allowed to enter their lives? She had been sexually assaulted; and Job had lost his wealth, his children, his health, his friends' respect, and even his wife told him to curse God and die (Job 1–2). These were not glowing invitations for trusting in God's faithfulness and I wondered, "Were these people crazy?"

Increasing doubt and confusion came as I encountered Job at the end of the book giving praise and glory to God through his tragedy. It was one thing to endure the pain and suffering, but to actually praise God for it seemed ridiculous. Again, I wondered, "Am I missing something?"

৯০

Desperation is an interesting thing, leading us to do things we would otherwise believe inconceivable. After months of watching my marriage and family slowly falling apart, coupled with reading Job and the story from the woman on the radio rattling around in my head, I finally succumbed to the overwhelming desperation I felt about my life. I dared to do the unthinkable. I dared to hope Jesus could help and that God would intervene.

I rationalized for a long time how this might happen but, of course, came up empty. The only thought I had was, "Surely it can't get as bad as Job." It was in that moment I took the step that would forever change the course of my existence. One Monday morning, about 5:00 a.m., in the silence before anyone arrived at work, I got down on my knees in my office, hands on the floor in front of me to steady my shaking body, and prayed what I believe to be the scariest prayer a person can ever pray. "Okay, Lord, whatever you have to do to save my family, do it."

When I said the words, I meant them, but honestly had no idea what I was really praying. All I knew was I was desperate for God's help, whatever that might look like.

Roughly three weeks from the day I prayed that prayer, Todd would come home and confess to having an affair with a woman at work. I was devastated.

There are no words to describe the sucker punch in the gut I felt by Todd and God that evening. I had not seen this coming and truthfully felt betrayed by both. But whose betrayal was worse? Todd had broken our marriage vows, but we both willingly entered into those. God had been enticing me to this place of hope and surrender my whole life, and this is how he rewards me? He gets me to pray for "whatever" from his lofty throne and then destroys me?

This event was the single most defining moment of my life to that point, shattering everything I trusted and held dear to my heart—my marriage, my family, my faith, my identity, my idea of hope, and my relationship with Jesus. In one fell swoop, the Creator allowed all my illusions to be completely shattered.

At the time, I had no idea the view of these things I held so dear was wrong or the places of prominence they had in my life were so off-balance until they all came crumbling down around me. But as I sat there in the Burger King parking lot, only twelve hours after everything had been shattered, the invitation from Jesus came to live in truth rather than illusion and to actually engage the hope for which my heart so longed.

But could I? And even if I thought I possibly could find hope, was I willing to accept the invitation to trust Jesus with what I held most dear and surrender the outcomes to him after all that had happened?

Though I didn't know it at the time, this was my invitation to begin surrendering everything, starting with my marriage, to God in the hopes that his son, Jesus, would sustain me regardless of the end result. My choice would mark the beginning of an entirely new way of living with Jesus and I had no idea that this one decision would eventually lead to a life of surrendering...*everything*.

2

Abandoning God

*The story of your life is the story of the
long and brutal assault on your heart
by the one who knows what you
could be and fears it.*

—John Eldredge,
Waking the Dead

I had already abandoned God once. How had I allowed myself to get sucked back into the idea of trusting this invisible God, only to be hurt again? The first time I was just a child, so I can give myself some leniency for that mistake, but this time, I was a rational, intelligent adult with a fully formed brain. How had I been so stupid?

A familiar mantra I'd heard growing up chimed in my ears. "Hurt me once, shame on you. Hurt me twice, shame on me." (Deep, guttural sigh.) Yes, shame on me indeed.

ॐ

I grew up in a small town in rural Missouri. It was the kind of town where nothing much ever really happened, and everyone seemed to know each other and their business. Growing up in a town like this, it felt like there were only two extremes—you were either super religious, engulfing yourself in church life *or you* wanted nothing to do with God. In hindsight, I'm sure there were variations in between, but from my limited perspective as a child, these were your only two choices.

The home I grew up in battled between the tensions of these two extremes as my mom followed Jesus and my dad did not. I don't remember him being antagonistic about this (at least not in front of me), but I also never remember him stepping foot in church with us or mentioning God. Regardless of his beliefs, my mom made sure that me and my two younger siblings were in church every Sunday morning, every Sunday evening, and every Wednesday evening for fellowship dinner and teachings.

I remember those days so fondly as it was during one of those Sunday evening services when I came to confess Jesus Christ as my Savior at the age of twelve. Even now I can close my eyes and experience the moment quite vividly, like it was yesterday. Every detail burned into my memory as the evening encapsulated such great joy and such great confusion all at the same time.

The pastor had preached such a profound sermon on God and his desire to be in a relationship with people through his son Jesus that I was captivated. The way he spoke, it was as if he really knew this Jesus he was talking about and made him seem so present and tangible. I found myself deeply wanting to know this Jesus he was talking about. As the message came to a close and everyone bowed their heads to pray, he extended the invitation. "If anyone would like to invite Jesus into their hearts and lives, wherever you are, with your eyes closed, repeat this prayer after me…" I don't remember the specific words he prayed; all I know is that I repeated after him, meaning every word with my whole heart. At that moment, I had invited Jesus into my heart to be my Lord and Savior and I was beaming inside.

When the final "amen" was proclaimed, closing the prayer, the pastor smiled broadly from the pulpit, scanned the crowd, and very invitingly said, "Now if any of you prayed that prayer to ask Jesus into your life, be sure to come tell me before you leave."

I was a little giddy inside as I wondered, "What is going to happen now?" Supposedly, getting to know Jesus would change everything for me. Though I was extremely nervous, I couldn't wait to tell the pastor. I remember Mom going to get the car with my siblings and telling her I needed to go to the bathroom. I don't remember exactly why, but I wasn't ready to share what had happened with her yet. I think I just wanted to first share it with the man who had extended the invitation. So as she headed out, I hung back waiting for all the older folks to file out. (This was back in the day when small-town pastors would stand at the exit doors, shaking hands and exchanging prayer requests with the parishioners as they left service.)

Finally, it was my turn. I remember staring at my feet for such a long time before getting up the courage to actually look him in the eyes. When I finally did, he extended his hand to shake mine, and the words slowly and awkwardly flowed from my mouth, "I, umm, I just wanted to tell you, umm, for you to know that I prayed the prayer you said to ask Jesus into my heart tonight. You said to come tell you, so…" and that's all I could muster to say.

What came next confounded my young, new believing heart and, honestly, still does to this day. With little emotion and a half-hearted smile, he patted me on the back of my left shoulder with three small taps and said, "That's nice, be sure to tell your mom." He then turned his gaze to the adult behind me and began engaging them in conversation. Moving slowly toward the exit, I felt kind of dazed. What had just happened? I thought this was a big deal. Was it, or wasn't it? If it was such a big deal, then why the lackluster response? If it wasn't a big deal, then why had he made such a passionate display from the pulpit to get my response? I was utterly confused.

This moment marked the enemy's first assault on my young believing heart, casting immediate doubt on my belief in the significance of this Jesus I had just professed as my Savior. It would not be the last assault, but it was the most profound coming swiftly and harshly only moments after my confession and I was wounded.

Baptism was the next step once I'd shared with my mom about my profession of faith. I wasn't sure if it, too, would be another disappointing experience, but apparently, it's what you did once you accepted Jesus into your heart, so she signed me up. As it turns out, it was so much more than I ever could have imagined, and even now I reflect on that day with much fondness.

One of the parishioners in our church lived on a lovely piece of property with a large pond on their side yard. It was the perfect setting for a baptism. The terrain surrounding the pond was full of lush green grass and flowers that sloped slightly downward toward the water, allowing everyone to sit comfortably in lawn chairs and blankets with a great view of the festivities. There were also a few large trees to provide shade and covering, as it was a warm summer day in August.

I don't know the attendance (there were probably no more than fifty), but when I close my eyes, I remember all the people blanketing the edge of the water. There was such joy and excitement in seeing so many people gathered on the bank to witness my public profession of faith. I, of course, was not the only one being baptized that day, but when you're young, it feels like everything is focused on you.

Our senior pastor would be doing the honor of baptizing that day and I remember him standing out in the pond with water up around his waist as he began our baptism service. Again, from that older age of the church, he was wearing a short-sleeved button-up dress shirt with a tie, dress pants, and would preach a short sermon from the water before beginning the baptisms. While I don't remember what he said, I know I felt holiness and reverence for this ancient tradition we were about to engage.

Finally, the moment came when the baptisms would begin, but to my surprise, there was one more element the pastor wanted to incorporate before calling the people one by one into the water. Reaching down into his pocket, I saw him pull out a small glass bottle with a cork in it. Holding it up in the sky, the sunlight glimmered off the clear contents. He began to share with the crowd about his recent trip to Israel and how he had filled this bottle with water from the Jordan River. He spoke of walking where Jesus had walked and how we would now be baptized in the same water, which Jesus had been baptized. He then slowly poured the contents of the bottle into our little pond.

I was mesmerized and in awe. Was I about to be baptized in the same water that Jesus had been baptized in, really? I can't explain it, probably just my young mind at play, but somehow I felt like this added a new dimension to what I was about to do. Was there power in being in the same water as Jesus? Oh, I had hoped so!

The time finally came, and my name was called, so out into the water, I slowly waded. It was colder than I'd expected, and I hated the feeling of the mud squishing between my toes. Plus, then and now, I disdain being in water where I can't see what may be swimming around me, but I had to let that fear go for the moment at hand. Placing his right hand on my back, my pastor took the lead, looked me in the eyes, and asked me pointedly, "Steph, have you asked Jesus into your heart?" I nodded and whispered, "Yes." Then, I immediately crossed my arms in front of me, gripping my right wrist with my left hand and securely grasping and squeezing my nose with my right thumb and pointer finger.

His words were strong and full of authority, "I now baptize you in the name of the Father, and of the Son, and of the Holy Spirit." As he finished his last word, I tightly closed my eyes, grasped my nose harder, and then backward and under the water I went. Coming up from below the surface, I heard clapping, whistling, and a few people shouting "Amen!" My mom and grandmother were there, teary-eyed and glowing with pride. Dad didn't come, this wasn't his sort of thing, but it didn't matter. At that moment, my young heart was full and I was so happy I couldn't contain it. I remember at the time feeling like my cheeks were going to burst from smiling so big. It was a great moment!

We closed out the service by singing a few acapella worship songs, ending with "Amazing Grace," and then gathered around picnic tables filled with a fantastic potluck smorgasbord of food and desserts. Our church knew how to fellowship!

It truly was an exhilarating day and significant part of my faith journey, unmatched in many ways. But as exciting as the day was overall, I remember how I felt sitting there at the picnic table as the day came to a close. The sun was slowly setting, and people were beginning to clean up and gather their things. I remember looking out at the sun glistening on the now calm water and thinking to myself, "I don't feel any different. I wonder if that's normal?"

Another assault so soon after a spiritual victory, this one was more subtle, but the effects were the same…more doubt.

စာ

Divorce is an ugly thing. As a now ordained pastor and licensed professional counselor, I have yet to spend time with anyone who has actually gone through a good divorce. Some may be less fraught with drama, but the effects of dissolving a marriage are hard even if the divorce is a necessary and amicable thing. And no matter how hard people try, if there are children involved, the effects of the decision trickle down on them. This was my personal experience as well.

I can't remember if I was thirteen or fourteen years old at the time of the actual divorce, but I do remember that it wasn't long after my baptism that my parents' marriage began to unravel. Dad was a good-looking, athletic guy with a wandering eye and had, on many occasions, been unfaithful to his marriage with my mother. The last indiscretion was the final straw, and Mom felt she had no choice but to leave. At the time, this was undoubtedly the hardest decision she'd ever had to make, and she was full of confusion and doubt daily.

Witnessing the effects of her decision to end the marriage was extremely painful for me as a child. I watched helplessly as Mom sunk into a deep, debilitating depression, spending a lot of time laying on the couch, refusing to eat or go outside. At one point, she had physically dwindled to a mere ninety pounds. At such a young age, I was spending more than my fair share of time taking care of my siblings, then ages eight and nine, as Mom tried to emotionally stabilize.

On many occasions, my thoughts would turn to Jesus, wondering, "Where is he in all of this?" I mean, isn't he supposed to take care of those who follow him? Something seemed off with the whole "trust Jesus" business, but I had no one to help me wrestle through these questions as addressing Mom's emotional health had become more urgent than my discipleship as a follower of Jesus.

Eventually, Mom did pull out of the depression and began to engage in life again, but it took a long time. The divorce was finalized, and our family started to live in our new normal. It wasn't easy, but my siblings and I, with the help of our grandmother, linked arms with mom as a family and began to feel normal again. Interestingly, as we began to stabilize—Mom got a decent job, and we started doing more things as a family—we became more attractive to my dad. He began coming around a lot more than normal, and Mom seemed to welcome him, which was extremely confusing to me. I mean, why would she let him in after all that had happened?

I was not the only one confused during this time. Mom, too, was extremely conflicted. I know she wrestled with thoughts of what a good Christian should do. Wasn't it biblical to forgive? If there was a capacity to reconcile, shouldn't she do that to make our family whole again? The questions bombarded her as Dad continued to charm his way back into her heart, and she didn't know what to do.

At one point, Dad even proposed again, and they began to talk of remarriage. Mom had no choice but to seek wisdom and help from our church, so she made an appointment with her pastor. Sitting in his office, the tears flowed torrentially as she shared her questions and concerns. The bottom line was that no matter what my dad had previously done, she still loved him. My mother had been with my father all through high school and now had three children with him. Her love hadn't stopped because of his unfaithfulness or because they had divorced. She just wanted to know what to do. If she chose to reenter the relationship, what should she be aware of and how should she prepare? If she chose not to reenter it, how could she move past the pain and love she still felt for him?

To my shock and surprise, her sobbing questions were met only by a stone-faced, rigid disdain for my dad and my mom's consideration of restoration. The pastor would not mince words, as swiftly and directly he spoke, "Listen, your ex-husband is a cancer, and you know what you do with cancer. You cut it out."

Mom's bottom lip quivered as she responded, "But what if this was you and your wife, wouldn't you want to give her another chance?"

Smugly, he responded, "My wife would never do such a thing." There was nothing left for Mom to say or do, so she slowly rose and exited his office. The pastor just let her leave without saying another word or even offering prayer.

Once again, I was confused. I thought the church was a place where the love and grace of Jesus were supposed to be displayed? Where was Jesus and why were these representatives of his church doing so much damage to his people? More than anything, what my mom was looking for that day was to be supported. It was support, however, that did not come and I took note.

In the months to follow, it became clear that my father was still not really interested in engaging in normal family life, and Mom was able to finally let him go. There would be no remarriage to my dad, but the damage had been done by the pastor, and the church was never again a safe place for us as a family. Eventually, we quit going, which was fine by me.

At the time, I don't think I could have verbalized it, but between the first pastor's lackluster response to my proclamation of faith and the second pastor's response to my mom's marital struggles, I was done with the whole idea of following Jesus. I had trusted, took a leap of faith, and surrendered myself to Jesus that Sunday evening only twelve to fifteen months earlier, and for what? If I was experiencing how Jesus took care of his people, then I didn't need him. I could have a difficult life without him and not have to worry about following all of his rules.

Good riddance!

ço

Looking back, it's striking to me the lengths the evil one (yes, I do mean Satan and fully believe in his existence) was willing to go to destroy my blossoming faith and bring doubt. His attacks were immediate and swift with such precision in the exact areas of my young life that would cause the most damage to my faith. How calculating and devious are his ways.

Jesus didn't want anything from me at that time except my heart, so why was my young life such a target for the enemy? Because he knew before I did how precious my life was to God and what I could one day do for his kingdom if I ever gave him more than just my heart. If he destroyed my heart for Jesus as a child, there would be nothing else to surrender later, not anything.

3

Longing for Love

The fine flower of unholiness can grow only
in the close neighborhood of the Holy.
Nowhere do we tempt so successfully
as on the very steps of the altar.

—C. S. Lewis,
Screwtape Proposes a Toast

The problem with abandoning God is it left a gaping hole in my heart that only he was designed to fill. As an adolescent, I had no comprehension of this knowledge, only longing. It was a longing to be seen, to be valued, to be protected, and to be loved unconditionally. I had thought my initial profession of faith would lead to the fulfillment of these longings but instead what I found was disappointment.

I was so close to the truth and had begun to taste the goodness of God. I may not have wanted anymore to do with him, but my soul still longed for what only he could provide. In my rejection of God, the enemy saw an opportunity to twist my longings. If God was not going to fulfill them, then certainly someone could do it better and so my search began.

☙

The longing to be loved and noticed by my father was a constant battle for me as a child. It's not that he didn't love me, of this,

I am certain; it's that, during that season of his life, he loved himself more. He was always working, hanging out with friends, playing softball, or doing something that kept him away from home. I think he liked the idea of being a father but how to practically do it was so foreign to him; I guess it was just easier to stay away than to feel "less than."

I do have many fond memories of growing up and doing things with Dad, but only because that's what he was good at the "fun stuff." Otherwise, he was absent in the day-in-day-out drudgery of normal fatherhood. This, however, is where, as a young girl, I needed him the most. I needed an unconditional fatherly love that would correct me, protect me, and encourage me so when I entered the realm of dating later in life I would know what to look for in a young man. No such guidance came.

I began to feel the pain of my father's absence and protection a few years prior to my parents' divorce and would continue to feel it in the years that ensued. The wounding that came to my young heart during this season of life is difficult to put into words. It was a field ripe for the enemy to assault, leading me to harm that would in turn do further damage to my heart.

My earliest memories of living with my both parents were at our small three-bedroom ranch home in a subdivision full of kids. I had my own room with a white canopy bed adorned with pink tapestry around the top. In the backyard, we had a metal swing set I would spend hours on with my siblings. The biggest perk was that the entire neighborhood was on a large oval, which made it perfect for me to ride my bike in circles for hours. We were also located somewhat close to my elementary school, and by third grade, I was able to walk there by myself like the big kids. It was a fantastic setup.

To my disappointment, after a few years, my parents lost the house to foreclosure. The reasons why were not shared with me as a child, and even now I don't know the whole story. I guess it's not something my parents wanted to share with their child. Regardless of the why, the house was gone, and we ended up in an apartment for a while. Money was still tight, though, and eventually, when they could no longer make rent, to keep us from becoming homeless, my grandparents stepped in to help.

Dad's parents lived in a large ranch home on four acres out in the country. It was a beautiful home on a lovely property, and we were invited to live in the basement until my parents could get back on their feet. On the surface, this sounds extremely generous. However, for a then ten-year-old, the reality was unsettling.

The basement was only partially finished, meaning, there was some wood paneling over the concrete walls; otherwise, the only other finished walls were those surrounding the staircase leading into the basement. Our new home consisted of two open areas that flowed into one another. The living room area held our couches and a TV, which flowed to the dining table and then to the kitchen. You would then walk behind the stairs to our sleeping area, which consisted of one queen-sized bed and two twin beds all in the same open area. We had a few dressers, nightstands, and a metal cabinet to hang some clothes. To say it was not ideal is an understatement.

The element that angers me the most when I reflect on that period of time was our makeshift bathroom. For reasons unknown to me, my grandparents did not want us coming up and down the stairs to use the bathroom. We were allowed to go upstairs and use the bathroom in we had to go "#2"; otherwise, we need not bother them by running upstairs to pee. Instead, we were given a brown wooden portable toilet with a white, plastic, removable bowl. It was like a training toilet for adults. It sat out off to the side of our sleeping area, and when anyone had to pee, you would announce to everyone not to come over to that side of the basement—so shameful.

I guess I should be grateful that we had a warm, dry place to live. We were not homeless, but this would be another season of feeling "cast aside" by Dad.

If you count the number of beds, you quickly realize there isn't enough sleeping space for five people—this would be correct. As my siblings, mother, and I packed up and moved into our new basement home, Dad went to work in Louisiana. Initially, it was to be a short-time gig to get us back on our feet financially with the intention of him coming back to be with us as often as possible. In actuality, Dad ended up living there for two years, only returning home very sporadically. I felt like we had been forgotten.

I didn't know it at the time, but I was beginning to formulate a twisted narrative in my head of what marriage and family looked like that would later come back to bite me in my own marriage. Apparently, the woman did everything in a marriage and expected very little from her husband other than a paycheck. It makes sense if this is all you see. My mom was imitating for me what my grandmother had modeled for her. I would later fall into the same pattern.

∽

Statistics say that most sexual abuse comes to children at the hand of close friends or family. Professionally, I have found this to be true and believe it happens because these close relationships provide the proximity necessary for someone to spot and groom children who have no protection or who have a longing to be loved. This, too, would become part of my story.

A wife, no matter how strong she is, needs to be with her husband. This is the point of "leave and cleave"—to become one, found in Genesis 2:24 NIV. So several years prior to the divorce, when my mom had the opportunity to go spend a couple of weeks in Louisiana with Dad, she jumped at the chance. The problem, however, was what to do with three school-age children? Dad's parents loved us, but were definitely not up for the challenge. My mom's mother loved us as well and would have taken us in, but she worked the second shift, and this would be difficult to pull off. No worries, a couple from church were happy to take us in for a few weeks. They had several children close to our ages, and we all attended the same elementary school, so it would be easy to hop on the bus with them.

The husband was an extremely affectionate man who loved Jesus. I had never met anyone like him. He loved to talk and play with his kids. He prayed with them at night before bed, disciplined them when necessary, and was extremely loving and respectful to his wife. I had never seen this kind of a husband and father up close before. It was nice and made me feel safe.

This safety made me think nothing of it when he'd invite me to snuggle with him on top of the covers in his bed. It was always during the day, always with the door open, and always when his wife and children were in the living room or kitchen just beyond the walls of the bedroom. Surely, I thought as a kid, this is okay. But again, how would I know? I had no context for how a father and daughter should intimately connect. Maybe this was normal?

Unfortunately, the day things became "not right" was painfully obvious, however, I had no clue what to do. The extent had been inappropriate touching, but it was still wrong and made me feel nauseous inside. I thought this was someone, an adult male who *finally* saw me and cared for me. Now what? I evaded future opportunities for abuse the next few days by pretending I couldn't hear him when he called to invite me to "nap" or "rest" for a bit, but I feared how long I would be able to dodge his attempts.

As is typical with most pedophiles, fear of getting caught eventually kicked in when he realized I was no longer responding to his ruse, and so he quickly went into self-protection mode. I remember standing at the bus stop the morning he came out to talk to me before I got on the bus. "Hey, Stephy, I just wanted to talk to you real quick about what happened the other day. I was praying and God really laid it on my heart that what we [hear the pedophile language insinuating I had done something wrong as well] did was wrong. So I won't be inviting you to lay down with me anymore, okay? And you know, I'm really embarrassed about all of this, so let's just keep it between us. We wouldn't want my wife to get upset. Okay?"

At only ten years of age, what was I supposed to say? Of course, I nodded and said, "Okay." This would be the last time he gave me any attention, as the next week in their home, he treated me like I was invisible. This, too, would breed in my young heart proof that I was unworthy of love by adult men.

I'm surprised, in view of this horrific encounter with a Christian man, that I had any interest in the things of God as I grew up. However, I think this negative experience, alongside my feelings of rejection from my father, are what made me open to a relationship with God. My soul needed a man, a father figure in my life to show me what love, real unconditional love looked like. Clearly, no human man, even a Christian one, was capable of truly providing this, which is why two years later at the age of twelve, I jumped at the chance of a relationship with Jesus. The pastor that Sunday evening had portrayed a relationship with Jesus to be just the thing my heart needed, a way to God, an avenue to finally be seen, which is why it hurt so much when it didn't pan out as expected.

What does a child do with that kind of hurt, confusion, and disappointment?

The next two to three years after abandoning God had brought no further clarity or hope in the realm of feeling truly loved. Yes, my mom, dad, and grandparents all expressed their love for me, but deep in my soul, I still felt unseen and worthless. As I entered high school and the world of feeling daily judged by my peers, the desire to feel loved grew more intense and more necessary than ever before. This, too, would make my young heart a prime target for the enemy to strike, camouflaging more abuse with the appearance of real love.

The situation began innocently enough when a friend of the family, Bryan, started spending more time with us. I was fourteen years old at the time, on the edge of fifteen, and he was in his twenties. I'm certain, early on, what I felt was just a crush because I was always so excited to be around him. He actually looked at me when we talked and listened well. Men didn't do that in my life, so this was new and nice.

Bryan entering my life, only a few years after abandoning God, was like the heavens parting, and all the desires of my heart finally being fulfilled.

Over the next few months, he became a regular visitor in our home, so on New Year's Eve, when he asked my mom if he could take me to a movie, no one thought anything of it. For everyone else, this was viewed as nothing more than friends hanging out, but for me, it felt different. For me, this felt like a real date.

To my delight, the evening did not disappoint, being filled with fun, laughter, a passionate kiss, and my introduction to alcohol for the first time as he offered me a peach wine cooler on the way to the movie. I was a bit nervous at first, but wanting to seem *adult*, I took it and loved it. I don't ever remember feeling so happy. For the first time, everything felt like it was supposed to be. I was experiencing a real connection with a man, and I finally found a way, through alcohol, to relax. Over the next few months, our relationship quickly moved to a full-on sexual one, and at the tender age of fifteen, I was certain I was in love.

There were moments, though, when my heart would question things. I thought love, true, unconditional love, fought for the object of its affection. When our relationship turned physical, he was adamant that I go to the public health clinic to get on birth control. I was terrified. As a young girl, I had never received a gynecological exam, and now I was to go alone to a public clinic. When I raised my objections, I was told it was my choice, but that if I got pregnant, I would have to abort it. Again, my young mind fought to understand. Why would someone I loved put that kind of ultimatum on me? The thought also lingered, so what if I got on birth control and still got pregnant, would he try to make me get rid of a baby? I knew this was something I could never do, and yet the person I loved was saying that would be my only option. It didn't compute. Ultimately, because I loved him, I did what he asked me to do and went to the clinic. A sense of shame shrouded me that day as I felt so dirty.

During this time, glimmers of my previous faith began to spring up, wreaking more havoc in my young mind. The book *88 Reasons Why the Rapture Will Be in 1988* came out and was brought to our home by my grandmother. While I had no use for Jesus in my life, I will admit that the fear of "being left behind" if all that Jesus stuff was true brought me a lot of anxiety. Clearly, the book was fraudulent, but at the time, it made me stop to consider my life.

Bryan and I had never spoken about matters of faith, so I had no idea where he stood, but the fact that we were having sex and that abortion was on the table for him gave me some idea. I remember on a few occasions trying my best to explain my fears and discuss what I'd been taught growing up, but he blew it off as nonsense. I remember him saying, "Don't worry about it, if God is real I'll take the heat for anything bad you've done." I didn't know much, but I was pretty sure it didn't work that way.

We were actually able to keep our relationship hidden for quite a while, but when my mom found the birth control pills under my bed, everything blew up. Mom called Dad and there were lots of conversations about "statutory rape" and "reporting this to the authorities," but nothing ever happened. There was a brief period of time when we were forced to not see one another, but eventually, for reasons I still don't understand, my mom and dad allowed us to begin seeing one another again. I'm sure as a young, heartbroken teen, I fought for this, but in the years to follow, the enemy would use this piece of information to affirm my feelings of being unloved. I mean, if my parents wouldn't even fight for me when they thought what was happening to me was illegal, then something must be wrong with me—at least this is what my young adult heart would wrestle through for years.

It was actually when my relationship with Bryan was finally out in the open that things began to change. As a sixteen-year-old, I had lots of dreams for my future, but he was not on board for any of it. Talks about college were squashed, and it was being subtly revealed to me that after graduation, we would get married, have kids, and that I'd be happy being a wife. At the time, I still believed I loved him, but this was not the trajectory I had planned for my future.

It was still a few years away, so rather than cause fights, I just ignored the assumptions about our future together. Besides, in the meantime, I had a boyfriend who got me as much alcohol as I wanted. However, even this relational bonus began to sour as he tried to exert more and more control over the clothes I wore, the way I fixed my hair, and even how I cooked. Though I have no idea where it came from, I am grateful for an inner strength that welled up within me to not put up with this kind of behavior and eventually broke the relationship off.

Bryan, however, did not exit my life quietly. Over the next year, he would continue to bring me gifts, leave flowers and notes on my car, and show up at my place of work. Though I tried to nicely remind him we were over, his efforts only seemed to intensify. When I finally refused to engage in communication, things eventually stopped, but it took a while. Thankfully, I was finally able to move on.

"Move on"—what a strange, adult phrase for a seventeen-year-old to be using to describe a high school relationship ending. But that is what I had to do in that season. At seventeen years of age, I had to acknowledge for myself that I had not been in a healthy relationship, and in fact, that it was in many ways emotionally and sexually abusive. During this time, I also made the connection of how my dad's absence during childhood, and what had happened to me with the man from church at the age of ten, had set me up to be ripe for this kind of brokenness. Ugh, how had I become the girl with "daddy issues"? Well, at least I recognized it, but how to change would be a different story as I still desperately was longing for love.

The enemy had witnessed how close I'd come to being all-in with God when I was twelve years old, and he was now coming after me with a vengeance to make sure I didn't go back after abandoning him. These attempts to masquerade the love my young heart needed were powerful and, for brief seasons, effective. Thankfully, God was still fighting for me; I just didn't know it at the time.

4

Damaged

Consider the damage done to the
soul when the abuse is fused
with the legitimate longings of the heart.
The flower of deep longing for
love is somehow hideously intertwined
with the weed of abuse.

—Dan Allender,
The Wounded Heart

Abuse, whether we call it by name or choose to justify its harm with a lesser term, is still abuse. Its effects run deep and weave themselves into the heart of its victim in ways that are largely unseen. But make no mistake, these lurking monsters are there, waiting to rise up and devour anything that resembles happiness. Shame tells us we are just bad, maybe even leading us to justify our past abuses by the terrible mistakes we've made in the present. These lies are twisted and pervasive and yet they seem so true.

I had finally been given a special gift, the longing for which my heart so desired. Love. Unconditional, unequivocal love without reason or strings attached. All I had to do was receive it and reciprocate it, and yet I couldn't, not fully. Something in me had been broken and my longings damaged.

29

Without explanation or reason, I would sabotage the one thing I'd most longed for and lose my best friend in the process.

I remember the first day I saw Todd after summer break. It was our first day as high school freshmen. He was tall and thin, with dark olive skin, extra tanned from the summer sun, and biceps bulging from football practice. He had short, dark, spiky hair, and was wearing a short-sleeved button-up shirt with a collar. It was white with thick orange vertical stripes. He was so handsome and not at all like the young boy I'd met in eighth grade, all short and pudgy.

While we both knew of one another from the previous school year, Todd would later tell me it was my blue eye shadow that caught his attention our freshman year in math class. We quickly became an item and started "going out." I chuckle when I think about this term now as our dating relationship consisted of nothing more than him meeting me at my locker in the mornings and in between classes, and me walking him to the back of the building at the end of the day, where we would swap a quick kiss before he went to catch the bus for home. We were both fourteen at the time, and I believe our budding romance lasted all of four weeks before I met Bryan (from the previous chapter) and broke up with him. Todd didn't seem to be particularly devastated as the next week, he, too, had moved on to another romance himself. Ah, young love.

Todd and I had remained acquaintances the next few years of high school, running in similar friend groups. I was a cheerleader, and he was on the football and basketball teams. I wouldn't say either of us was popular, just connected enough to hang out on the fringe of popularity and be invited to the good parties. This social connection drew us closer as friends in our junior year of high school, as we both enrolled in a half-day technical school program. Every day around 11:00 a.m., we would load onto a bus from school that would take us to the technical school roughly twenty-five minutes away. The majority of kids on the bus hung out in very different circles than Todd and me, so our friendship grew deep quickly as we were together back and forth on the bus five days a week.

It's been more than thirty years since then, and while I can't remember the exact conversations we had on those bus rides, what I do remember is the way he made me feel. Todd could always make me laugh—belly laugh to the point of tears. It's strange to word it this way, but those bus rides were a sanctuary for me during a time when I was trying so hard to figure out how to get out of the relationship with Bryan. To sit and laugh with Todd made me feel normal and special. There was no desire to control or manipulate me, just a desire to make me happy. It was nice, but it was also foreign.

In hindsight, I believe these bus rides gave me a glimpse of what dating should be like, full of laughter and friendship building. In the end, our friendship is what gave me the courage to finally end the relationship with Bryan and "move on." I didn't end that relationship to be with Todd per se, I just knew that I really liked the way I felt when I was around him or when I thought I might get to see him.

These feelings with Todd were new and different than I'd ever experienced before. For starters, he was my age, which made the relationship feel right somehow. I knew I wasn't looking for a "father figure" in him, and I wasn't seeking attention or even love. For the first time ever, what I felt was genuinely being seen and known. I had a real friend, a true friend, and dare I even say, a best friend.

I believe that high school romance is unparalleled to any other relationship in life. The feelings are so deep during a time when our brains are not fully developed and ready for them. So when Todd and I crossed over from friendship into dating, we fell in love fast and hard. We officially became a couple midjunior year and were basically inseparable the following summer and into our senior year of high school.

He was such a romantic. I had boxes and boxes filled with love notes he would pass to me in school or leave on my car at work. One night, we spent several hours talking on the phone (you know back when there were home phones) dreaming together about our future as adults. We talked about where we would live…in a log cabin next to a stream and many other silly youthful longings. The next week, to my surprise, he brought me a poster compiled of pictures he'd clipped from magazines depicting the life we'd talked about on the phone that night. It was cheesy but so thoughtful and loving.

He even got fired from his job at Dairy Queen over me. I was ordering food in the drive-through during one of his shifts, and he heard my voice over the speaker so he ducked out the back door to sneak a quick kiss. Unfortunately, the owner was there that day, saw him, and fired him for being unprofessional. Thankfully, being that Todd was such a hard worker, the owner gave him his job back, but Todd wasn't fazed by it either way. This is the kind of love Todd gave me—unconditional and unrestricted by anything or anyone.

I, too, did my best to love him well, writing love notes and leaving him special gifts. At the time, our favorite food was Taco Bell and the nearest one was twenty-five minutes away in a larger town. I remember shopping with my mom one Saturday afternoon while he was at football practice and bringing him tacos back to leave in his car for him to find after practice.

I think the epitome of our silly love was during basketball season. Todd had played for three years, and I'd assumed he would play our senior year as well. I was done with the whole cheerleader scene after three years of it but tried out again anyway so I could travel to the games with him. Unknown to me, he didn't go out for basketball that year, but since I had made the cheerleading squad for him, he came to every game, even the ones far away to be there with me. He couldn't ride the bus since he wasn't on the team and sometimes drove for hours to away games. This is how we loved one another…fully, unconditionally.

During these early years of young love, the monsters of brokenness and abuse were lurking. While Todd loved me so well, it couldn't make up for the sense of shame and guilt I felt inside or my lack of self-worth. At the time, I made no connection to my past abuse. I just knew in certain moments I felt so very uncomfortable in my own skin. Thankfully, I knew how to handle this issue.

The drinking that had begun in my relationship with Bryan continued in my relationship with Todd. Though my avenue to buy alcohol had ended, I was lucky enough to get a job where I cleaned condos and villas at a country club. Every night I'd clean out rooms with all kinds of alcohol left behind. It was a veritable supermarket of booze left for a high school kid to pilfer, and boy did I! It was not uncommon for me to sneak garbage bags full of beer bottles into the trunk of my car after a Friday night shift. I would be set for an entire weekend, and the uncomfortable feelings would stay at bay…until they wouldn't.

Alcohol gave me a personality and boldness I felt was glaringly absent in my normal day-to-day interactions with people. It allowed me to say and do things that sober Stephanie would never even consider. On most occasions, this seemed like a good thing, but as my senior year progressed, it was clearly not.

I was seventeen at the time and rumors of things my ex-Bryan was saying about Todd and I began to surface and reach me. I didn't know if they were true, but still, they enraged me, and I decided I was not going to put up with that sort of thing. So after downing three or four beers, I got the liquid courage to drive to Bryan's apartment, nearly forty-five minutes away, to confront him. Of course, on the drive, I continued to drink, so by the time I arrived in his city, I was lit. In my inebriated state, I could not find his apartment building, so my *drunk wisdom* convinced me the local police station would be the best place to get directions. Somehow, I was able to find it and speak clearly enough to get directions from the officer at the front desk. Unfortunately, I was not coherent enough to follow the directions given (pre-smartphone and GPS days), so I went back to the police station and said I couldn't find it. (Yes, I was that stupid.) Thankfully, another officer on duty was willing to personally escort me over.

Following the police car, I drove a few blocks when he put on his left blinker to alert me, we had reached the apartment building. There was a narrow entrance leading into the parking lot that went over a small ravine, so of course, when I went to pull in, I landed my mom's car on the driver's side in the ditch. Sitting there in a daze, I watched as the officer slowly walked over, opened my car door, now wedged in the mud, and shined his flashlight in on me. Squinting my eyes in the light, I heard him address me by my mother's name (clearly, he had already run my license plates). He continued, "Ma'am, I'm gonna need you to step out of the vehicle and repeat your ABCs for me." With my head down, I told him my name was Stephanie, this was my mom's car, and that I was drunk. Nicely, he replied, "Yeah that's what I thought," as he helped me out of the ditch and placed me in the back of his patrol car.

I honestly don't remember much after getting into the patrol car. The next thing I knew, I was waking up on a couch in the police station with a trash can by my head. Apparently, I had thrown up at some point. The embarrassment continued when the officer then called my mom. God's grace was undeservedly present in the situation as no charges were pressed and as a drunk seventeen-year-old, I received no DUI or minor in possession charge. At the time, I just felt lucky, but today, I see it quite differently.

One would think that an event like this would be a turning point, but human brokenness in the hands of an enemy bent on destroying God's image in us is a powerful tool. Yes, of course, I was making terribly poor choices but the evil one was right there capitalizing on every moment of it. He was not about to let me go without a fight.

Not long after the evening in the police station, I remember having a conversation with my then-best girlfriend. It was a few hours before the Homecoming football game and we were at my house hanging out in the kitchen. I had never before admitted to anyone that maybe alcohol was a problem for me, but at the moment, it seemed like I could. I mean this was someone I considered to be a good friend, surely I could share my heart.

I remember the evening so clearly. She was sitting on the counter, legs dangling in front of the lower cabinets, leaning forward a bit on her hands. The conversation was easily set up as she asked if there was any alcohol in the house we could drink before heading out (Mom wasn't home at the time). Hesitantly, fidgeting, I looked at my feet and then made eye contact saying, "Well, there is, but I'm thinking that maybe I shouldn't drink anymore, or at least maybe I should cut back. What do you think?" The words that came next cut deep and resounded in my young soul for years. There was no pause and no hesitation in her response as she said quite emphatically, "Why would you do that, Steph? You know that no one likes you when you're sober."

Even now as I type these words, the tears come, and my heart breaks for that younger version of me who didn't stand a chance. I so just wanted to be loved and valued for who I was, yet my closest girlfriend was telling me that none of that was possible without alcohol. The way God made me, I was apparently not good enough, and I believed the lies. So I did what anyone would do. I caved under the pressure to be liked and continued to drink in an effort to feel normal.

ॐ

I somehow made it out of high school without another drinking-related incident. I actually attribute this to Todd as midsenior year he threatened to end things if I didn't cut back. I definitely didn't want to lose him, so for a while, this fear was an incentive to help me maintain a functional level of alcohol abuse. Unfortunately, love for someone else is never the catalyst to make someone stop addictive behavior, and I would eventually destroy things.

Graduation came, and at the age of eighteen, I moved out of my mom's house and in with a couple of high school friends. Freedom. It was so much fun. There were four of us, and we shared a two-bedroom apartment in a midsized town about twenty-five minutes from where we all had grown up. Away from family and the prying eyes of our hometown, we all got jobs, and two of us even tried college for a bit, but mostly, what we did was party. My roommate was the older sister of one of the girls I'd graduated with, and she was over twenty-one so we were set.

On the weekends, we'd have lots of people over or find someone else who was having a party. The town we were in had a community college where a lot of our high school friends attended, so there was always something to do. But it was more than just partying for me, even normal everyday activities weren't fun without alcohol. So we'd make it a point to buy beer before a trip to Aldi's or Sam's Club. I mean, life was supposed to be fun, right? We weren't hurting anyone. At least that's what I told myself at the time.

Todd was attending a technical college about an hour away, and we would see each other on the weekends during this year, so I don't think he really knew the extent of the way I lived. On the weekends, after a long week of school, he was ready to cut loose and have fun too, so I don't think it occurred to him that this was going on for me through the week as well.

My friends and I stayed at that apartment for a year and then decided to move back to an apartment in our hometown. Our number dwindled to three of us, partly because of how I interacted with one of the roommates. I won't blame my drinking, but I don't think it helped.

Our new place was nice and fresh, but the partying stayed the same and I began to unravel. The love I'd felt from Todd early on seemed so distant with him away at school and all my old longings to be seen and loved came rushing in with a vengeance. It didn't seem to matter that we were still together or that he continued to express his love to me in sacrificial ways. My heart was damaged, and I just wanted the hole I felt in my chest for love to be filled.

So when a middle school crush came back into my life, my heart was ripe for an unhealthy choice. At the time, I justified "flirting" as okay. I mean, I wasn't married and words are innocent enough. The problem is when I shared with certain friends about my conversations and flirting, what I got was twenty-year-old wisdom. "Just go for it, you were meant to be happy. Besides, you're not married, no one has to know." I wish I could tell you my great love for Todd and underlying moral compass were enough to help me make the right decision, but it did not, and eventually, I crossed the line.

I did not set out to be unfaithful to Todd or to hurt him. I know most people say that when they cheat, but I believe it's true a majority of the time. No one sets out to destroy their lives; they just want to dabble as close to the fire as possible in the hopes they won't get burned. This never works, and my world quickly went up in flames.

Christmas Day 1992, a few friends decided that "Todd needed to know" what I'd done and shared with him of my unfaithfulness. It was a blowup of epic proportions, leaving a hole in one of our apartment walls, ugly, mean, bitter words being yelled at me, and eventually the ending of our relationship. I. Was. Devastated.

In the weeks and months that followed, my drinking and poor choices would not only continue but escalate with now new levels of pain that needed to be numbed. Shame, self-hatred, and loneliness filled my soul and left me with so much loneliness. It wasn't just that I had lost my boyfriend; I knew I could find someone else to date if I wanted. No, what took me to the depths of darkness was the knowledge that I had lost my best friend, the only friend to this point in my life who had truly, unconditionally, without pause or hesitation loved me, all of me, the jacked-up broken me. I had destroyed that friendship and love because I was damaged and this knowledge utterly crushed me.

જી

Thoughts about my high school years are what give me the most confidence that God never lets go of us once we've truly, fully believed in his son Jesus with all our hearts as I did that night at the age of twelve. There was so much I did during that season of life to hurt my relationship with God, Todd, my friends, family, and myself; and yet, God still continued to send his Holy Spirit to lovingly convict and try to draw me back to himself. I felt his nudge to quit drinking, to stop having sex, and to get back into church on so many occasions. It was not condemning or heavy-handed, just a nudge that I was better than the choices I was making. In every area, I would try for a while, but I always got sucked back into my old ways.

When I think back to those early days of dating, I am in awe of how well Todd loved me, even at my worst. He had no faith background of his own that informed his decisions, just genuine love for me. His family never went to church and the experiences they did have with Christians up to that point had not been all that great. Still, he was open and willing to have discussions with me on the topic of God. I even gave him a Bible our senior year as a gift. He had to have thought I was crazy. The way I lived and the choices I was making clearly had no bearing or connection to faith or God. In hindsight, this, too, was a brilliant enemy strategy keeping Todd shut off from thinking God had any real influence on someone's life. My betrayal would send him even further away from God's influence and further damage my longing to be loved.

Still, God was working...

5

Skewed Perspective

When all you see is your pain,
you lose sight of me. (Papa)

—Wm. Paul Young,
The Shack

Pain, whether emotional, mental, physical, or spiritual, has a way of distorting our view. It is all-consuming and demanding, calling us to see people, events, and even God through its skewed lens. It is relentless and you had better believe the enemy will jump on its attempts to further pull us away from the heart of God any chance he can get.

My pain had taken me to depths of internal darkness and relational sabotage that I never could have expected at only twenty years of age. Emerging would not be easy but something in me desperately wanted to fight for the things I'd lost...for Todd. In hindsight, I know this was God at work in me, I just didn't know it was him at the time. Leaning into the fight, I would find my thoughts surprisingly being drawn to God, but in unhealthy skewed ways. I knew just enough about God from my younger days to be dangerous to myself. The enemy would use this knowledge against me in my pain and draw me further into a life that would settle for being treated poorly because that's what my pain said I deserved.

୭

The months following the breakup with Todd were brutal, and my ability to function continued to deteriorate. I was drinking all the time, isolating myself from friends and family, and eventually quitting a really good job as a graphic designer because I could not handle having to be somewhere at 7:00 a.m. every day. My twenty-year-old mind justified wanting to be free and adventurous, but the truth is, my inner turmoil made it impossible to believe I deserved anything good, even a job.

The next few months would be chaos as I jumped from job to job, trying to make ends meet. I tried selling dishes and kitchen wares door to door…horrible failure. The introvert in me cringes now that I even thought this was a viable opportunity. I attempted telemarketing, which was an even worse failure as I'd cry after every call that had taken me ten minutes to even attempt in the first place. Finally, I landed as a cashier in the convenience center of a local truck stop. It was definitely not a dream job, but it paid the bills and gave me something to do for a brief period of time. In the end, however, I would sabotage this as well.

Cell phones weren't really a thing yet at this point in 1993, at least not for the average person, so when I would isolate, there was no real way for anyone to check in on me. The day I lost the convenience store job was the day my eyes were opened to the pain I was not only inflicting on myself but others as well. I had left my apartment and decided to crash at my mom's for a few days. I just needed to be in a different space for a while, away from the partying and drinking. In and of itself, this was not a bad choice, except I didn't tell my roommates where I was going. I also had decided during this time, it would be nice not to go to work for a while, but I didn't bother to call in sick or explain why either.

I remember so clearly the day the realization of my self-destructive choices came to the surface. I was laying in my mom's queen-sized bed, engulfed in covers, staring at the ceiling. All was quiet as she and my siblings had left for work and school. I thought to myself, *Is this really my life?* Right about that time, the phone rang, and on the other end was one of my roommates yelling, "Where the hell have you been! Your work keeps calling here and is worried sick. They think something has happened to you. What is up with you?"

I gave no explanation but simply responded, "I'll take care of it," and hung up.

It's funny how small things can cause such a major shift. This moment was one of those things as my friend's call had awakened me to my selfishness. I had just needed time and space but took no consideration of how others were being impacted by my choices and in that moment I woke up…a little.

I mused in my head, "What is the right thing to do here?" I could call work, but that was me wanting to avoid conflict and increase my distance from the problem I had created. I knew this was not the answer, so I quickly dressed and drove to the truck stop. Walking in under a cloud of shame, I went to my boss's office to show I was indeed alive and to apologize for not showing up. While appreciative of my efforts, my boss still let me know that I was fired. I was not surprised by the company's decision and left feeling for the first time, in a long time, I had actually made a good choice.

The next few months were difficult, but I was determined to keep making better choices for myself. The first thing I did was build a resume with my graphics background and begin looking for a job. At the time, graphic design was still a budding career path, so it wasn't as easy as I'd hoped to find an entry-level job. Living in a small town, I found myself having to apply to jobs forty-five minutes to an hour away if I wanted anything in that field. Finally, after a few months, a break came, and I was granted an interview with a tiny sales and marketing company an hour from my apartment that paid $5.50 an hour. The drive alone would take up a considerable chunk of time and gas money, but it was an opportunity so I jumped at it.

The interview went fabulously, and I was confident my luck was about to change. I was told that it would be roughly a week before the company would make their decision, but I had no doubt

I would be their choice (gotta love early-twenties optimism). I had connected so well with one of the owners who interviewed me. He was a native New Yorker transplanted in St. Louis and looked just like Danny DeVito, only with white hair. He had a daughter about my age who lived back in New York, and there seemed to be a fondness for me beyond my skill set that I definitely felt was to my advantage. So it sent me spiraling the day he called to tell me the company had gone with another applicant. I was so crushed. I had put myself out there and look what happened…nothing. Rejection.

I remember commiserating about this with my mom on the phone after I had received the bad news. She had been very supportive and encouraging in my search and was disappointed as well that the job didn't work out. During this season of my life, she never pushed God on me, but this day, she chose to subtly remind me, "Don't get discouraged, Steph, God has something for you." I wasn't really sure what to do with that thought, so I simply replied, "I hope so."

The truth is, while it was a nice "mom gesture" of encouragement, I didn't quite believe in the efficacy of what she said. How could God have anything for me after all the poor choices I'd made? I remember getting off the phone, laying on my bed, and staring at the ceiling for hours wondering, "Now what?"

Lying there, I began to think about God for the first time in a very long while. Could he help me with this? Of course, he could, I knew enough about him to be certain that he *could* do anything. No, the question wasn't could he, but *would* he help me? I mean, was he even paying attention to my broken life? I seriously doubted it but ultimately decided I had nothing to lose, so why not send up a prayer. I don't remember what I said. My guess is it was short, sweet, and to the point with little hope or expectation. Still, I rationalized, it was an effort.

With this kind of radical disbelief in God's desire to help me, I could not have been more shocked when two weeks later, I got a call from the same company who rejected me, asking if I'd still be interested in the job. What? Before committing to anything, I went back for another interview at which time I was told the previous person hadn't worked out. The brash little New Yorker then proceeded to tell me how much he liked me and that I had been the first choice for the position, but because of my drive and my age, he didn't think I'd be dependable. It was slightly insulting, but in hindsight, he was absolutely seeing the truth of who I was at the time and had initially made a wise decision. Regardless of how it came together, it all worked out for both me and the company. Never underestimate the power of desperate prayer.

Driving home from the interview, offer and start date in hand, I wondered, *Was God in any of this?* My rational brain quickly interjected, *Of course not, the company is desperate and you were the only one available. End of story.* Logically, this made sense to me, but in my heart, I wasn't quite convinced.

Whether God had been helping me or not, my new job gave me the confidence to keep reaching out to Todd. For six long months, we had been broken up. We both dated other people during that time, but hope remained for me as every three or four weeks I'd get him to spend time with me. It would always end in a sexual encounter, which initially made me feel like we were somehow rebuilding intimacy, but restoration of the relationship never came. How twisted and quick my young heart was to believe sex meant love. Whether real or perceived, at least for those brief moments my heart felt close to him so I would continue to take whatever "love" I could get.

In time, I came to see that things were not going to be mended, so I made the request for one last "date" to at least have closure. We grabbed a quick dinner and then went to the movie theater, not sure what we would see. In hindsight, I think the idea of a movie was a safe choice because we would "technically" be together but not have to talk. There was only one movie starting when we arrived, so without a clue of what it was about, we purchased tickets and went in to see *Indecent Proposal* with Demi Moore and Woody Harrelson.

If you are not familiar with the movie, the quick story is that Demi and Woody are married and are in a considerable financial bind. On a whim, they decide to go to Vegas and try gambling as a way to fix their problem. This backfires, and they find themselves left without hope. In the midst of all this, a wealthy businessman becomes enraptured with Demi and offers her husband, Woody, one million dollars to spend one night with her. Together the couple agrees, trying to convince themselves that it's just sex and won't mean anything. However, the rest of the story is how this event wreaks havoc on their marriage, ultimately destroying it.

About a third of the way into the movie, there is this intense scene where Woody realizes what he has agreed to and is desperately trying to stop the events he has placed in motion. His feelings are so palpable, and you can almost feel his pain through the screen. I looked over and tears were streaming down Todd's face. I reached over and tried to hold his hand, but he quickly snapped it away from me and got up, leaving the theater. Shame, such intense shame, flooded over me at that moment as I realized on a deeper level than ever before how my betrayal had broken his heart.

To my surprise, ten to fifteen minutes later, Todd did return, and we finished the movie. Afterward, we didn't speak, but simply left the theater, got into the car, and drove back to his parents' house where he was staying. The car ride was eerily silent. The movie had been very difficult to watch and stirred up so much pain inside of both of us. But in the end, it left us more perplexed because regardless of what had happened, Demi and Woody chose each other and decided to make things work.

Pulling into the driveway, we remained silent as Todd put the car in park. Neither of us knew what to say or do, so we sat there for a long time in the dark, staring forward at the garage door in front of us, illuminated by the dusk to dawn light above. This wasn't quite how I had envisioned our last date together and had no idea what to say or how to leave. So with tears welling up in my eyes, I finally turned to look at him. When I did, he, too, looked over at me, tears in his eyes as well. He managed a very small smile and then reached over and took my hand. In a very low whisper, I then heard the words, "I still want to be with you."

With a sigh of relief and through a clenched throat, I responded, "Me too."

❧

What's important to know about that night so long ago is that when Todd and I decided to get back together, we never talked about what I had done. *Never.* We never talked about the pain I had caused him, the reasons why I had done it, or anything surrounding the betrayal. We had made the decision to put it behind us and attempted to move forward as if it had never happened.

The problem is, you can't push pain down far enough that it ever goes away. It is always there, lurking beneath the surface, waiting for the most inopportune time to explode all over your life if you don't deal with it. We didn't know it at the time, but Todd's pain from my betrayal was always lurking, and it would immediately begin to infiltrate our new relationship in harmful ways.

❧

My heart was so full of joy to finally have Todd back in my life for good that I chose to overlook how differently he treated me. My fun-loving, goofy, best friend was no longer present. Instead, what remained was someone who was emotionally distant, sharp, and hurtful with his words, and sometimes very uncaring in his interactions with me. I justified his behavior thinking I deserved to be treated this way after all I had done to him, hopeful that one day the old Todd would return.

If things had moved forward differently for us, I may have eventually stood up for myself, but about two months into our being back together, I would find out I was pregnant. Even in the midst of the dysfunction of our relationship, we were both happy about the news. Yes, it was a definite surprise, but we felt ready to move forward and build a family. So we bought a house and moved in together when I was seven months along in the pregnancy.

This season of my life was very much fraught with inner turmoil. On the one hand, I was thrilled to be with Todd (even though the relationship was tense), have a home, and a child on the way. On the other hand, I began to have all kinds of fears about how God viewed me and what he might do to me or my unborn child.

During this season, many distorted views and narratives about God began to filter into my mind. Todd and I were living together and having a child without being married. How might God punish me for these choices? Would he somehow harm my unborn child to teach me a lesson? Would he cause me to die in childbirth? Would something happen to Todd and me be left alone with a baby? So many negative thoughts flooded my mind daily, none based in truth, but I knew just enough about God to believe that my thoughts could possibly be right.

What should I do? Against all rationale, I decided to pray. I thought, even if God was mad at me, maybe he would be kind to my child. My mama's heart was already beginning to form, trying to keep my unborn child safe. So daily, for the last two months of my pregnancy, I would pray. I would pray for a safe delivery and for a healthy child. I would pray for God not to punish my baby because of my mistakes, and on a few occasions, I even prayed for his help to get my life back on track for the sake of my child.

The sentiment of prayer was all well and good, motivated by love for my unborn child, but as soon as our daughter was born healthy, my prayer life once again ceased. Maybe God had answered my prayer, and maybe I had just gotten lucky enough to have a healthy child. How could I ever really know? The answer didn't really matter because now I had my relationship, my child, a home, and a good job. What did I need God for now anyway?

I wasn't brazenly trying to deny God's possible presence in my life after our daughter was born, I simply had no idea how real or present in my life he might possibly be. So I attempted to move forward in a fog of maybes. Maybe God is real and listening; maybe he is not. Maybe God is mad at me for my life choices thus far;

maybe he is not. Maybe I should try to go back to church; maybe it doesn't even matter. In a sea of foggy maybes, I simply decided to do nothing and just kept trying to move forward with life.

ᔰ

Roughly four months after our daughter Sydney was born, Todd would come home and surprise me with a ring, asking me to marry him. It was a beautiful ring and a very sweet, simple proposal. I was sitting on the end of the bed, and he had reached into his top dresser drawer, pulled out the ring, bent down on one knee, and asked me if I would be his wife. Of course, I immediately said yes! We had decided when we first heard the news of my pregnancy not to get married simply because we were having a baby but to wait until the time felt right. I had, in faith, trusted this day would come and put Todd's last name on our daughter's birth certificate when she was born, hopeful that one day we would all share the same. In hindsight, that seems so risky, especially with all the unknowns in our relationships, but all worked out, and we would officially become the Ehmke family on October 1, 1994.

The events leading up to our marriage brought so much into question for my young, faithless heart about God and his people. Our engagement was short, only three months because I wanted a fall wedding and wasn't willing to wait another full year. Everything came together very quickly and effortlessly, except for the church piece. Call after call after call I made to so many churches but no one would marry us because we had a child and were living together. In a fit of rage, after a day full of rejection, I remember yelling at one pastor, "We are trying to make this right! Why won't any of you church people even help us?" Before he could answer, I hung up, frustrated and confused. My mind quickly darted back to my mom's divorce and the way her pastor had treated her, as well as the pastor who failed to be excited about my salvation decision. Irritatingly I reminded myself, "Yep, there it is, God's people still treating others poorly, this is why I don't go back to church."

Thankfully, the pastor at my mom's new church home during this time period was a nice guy, and he offered to marry us if we'd meet him for pastoral counseling. I wasn't exactly sure what to expect, but it definitely wasn't what we got. The interaction may have lasted fifteen minutes. There were no questions about our spiritual lives or where God may fit into our marriage. Just a few welcome pleasantries, questions about the wedding itself, and one question he wanted us to answer. Sternly he asked, "What are the two of you going to do if this doesn't work out?"

I remember us looking at each other, and then looking back at the pastor, both of us shrugging our shoulders when Todd spoke, "Well, it has to work out. We'll make it work."

The pastor smiled and warmly replied, "That's all I needed to hear." He then shook our hands, told us he'd be in touch about the specifics of the day, and that was the end. As we walked out, Todd was elated, so grateful that the conversation had been so quick and painless. I, on the other hand, was disappointed. Wasn't this "man of God" supposed to make sure we were ready for marriage? Wasn't he supposed to dig around and ask us hard questions about finances, extended family, raising kids, and having God in our home? It was so very subtle, but the seeds of doubt in God's love for me continued to grow through this experience. I mean, if God loved and cared for me, he would make sure his people at least tried to point me and my family to him, right? Clearly, I wasn't worth fighting for by God.

The first year of marriage was not the sea of bliss that so many describe. We'd already been living together for about seven months and had our daughter, so the days after the wedding were just like any other. The only difference was now we had a piece of paper. The old Todd that I still very much missed had not yet reemerged, and while disappointing, didn't seem to matter in the big scheme of things. I rationalized to myself, "I should just be grateful that he wanted to marry me and help me raise our daughter after all I'd done."

For the most part, I could live with this rationale until the days when I couldn't. My birthday in our first year of marriage glaringly stands out. Early on in our dating relationship, Todd had always surprised me with beautiful gifts on special occasions and sometimes simply for no reason at all. Since we'd been back together, the surprise gifts had stopped, but surely, my birthday would be different. The morning of my birthday came and went with no gift and no card. No worries, he was probably just in a hurry to get to work. All day at work, I sat in anticipation wondering if flowers or something special might arrive—nothing came. No big deal, flower delivery can be expensive, so maybe something special would happen later that night? Dinner came and went with no birthday movement. Finally, as we lay in bed around 11:00 p.m., with a single shred of hope left I said, "Any surprise birthday gifts for me over there? Maybe just a card?" (Surely, he was just leaving me in suspense.) With little expression, he looked at me and said in a very monotone voice, "No, I have nothing for you." He then reached over and turned out the light as I fell asleep in tears.

This kind of emotionally distant coldness was consistent during this season of our life, but there was just enough good that I kept justifying his behavior. For instance, we decided to have another child so our daughter could have a sibling. No one chooses to have a child with someone they don't love and respect, right?

We would get pregnant very quickly after making the decision to try, but this child would not grace our world. About eight weeks into the pregnancy, before I had even made it to my first OB–GYN appointment, I would begin to hemorrhage and lose the baby. My heart was broken. At the moment, Todd tried to be supportive, but only to an extent. He would take no time off of work or try to process with me the pain I felt over the baby we had lost. I was simply left to grieve alone.

During this time, I thought a lot about God and how I had stopped praying after our daughter was born healthy. Was he somehow punishing me now for my selfishness? All signs pointed to yes.

After a few months of physical healing, we began to once again try for another child, this time with no success. I mused internally, "Man, if God is real, he sure doesn't like me." We would keep trying for a year but had no luck, so we decided to put the baby stuff on hold and set our sights on the task of building a new home. The distraction proved to be good because not long into the process I found myself pregnant, once again.

I was, of course, terrified of losing this baby, so we kept the news close and only shared it with a few people until we were sure everything was going to be okay this time. With much relief, I made it to my first eight-week checkup, and all was well. We then scheduled a fourteen-week ultrasound to see the little Ehmke-to-be. I was so very excited. Our new home was coming along, Syd was growing like a weed, and in the next year, she would have a brother or sister. Life wasn't perfect, but there was much for which to be grateful.

The day of the ultrasound came, and with VHS tape in hand, I entered the doctor's building. There were no digital videos at the time, and Todd wasn't willing to take off work to go with me, so I was going to have it recorded for him. With much anticipation I lay on the table, watching as my doctor moved the camera around to see our little one. He would move the camera with one hand and use the other to move his computer mouse, making clicks on the video that came onto his screen. When he was all done, I sat up and waited for him to speak about what he saw. I was not prepared for what came as very empathetically he spoke, "Steph, I'm so sorry, the embryo is not there."

In disbelief, I stared at him. "I'm sorry, what?" was all I could muster.

He continued, "What you have is called a blighted ovum. You were pregnant, but after the fertilized egg implanted in the uterus, it did not develop into an embryo. Though the embryo did not grow, the gestational sac has continued to grow, which is why you still feel pregnant. Your body will eventually miscarry it, so there is nothing really for us to do at this point." I sat there in shock, all alone, hearing the worst news I had ever gotten at that point in life.

Todd was visibly more shaken with the news of this loss and attempted to bring comfort through flowers and nice gestures, but as was his pattern, he simply immersed himself in work rather than feel the pain and grief of this loss with me.

As the days and weeks moved forward, I began to feel mildly crazy. My body still had not miscarried the baby, and my abdomen continued to grow. I wondered, "Maybe the doctor was wrong? Clearly, my body says I'm still pregnant, so maybe I am?" I continued to eat healthy foods, take prenatal vitamins, and stay away from alcohol and over-the-counter medications as if I was still pregnant. Finally, after a month, I called my doctor and went in for another ultrasound. The verdict was the same and a DNC was scheduled to remove the blighted ovum.

Again, Todd would not take the time off work to go with me to the procedure, so my mom would take me. I was grateful for her support, but this was clearly a heartbreak; my husband was supposed to be there for me and yet he was not. Laying there in the recovery room after the procedure, I wondered, "How long am I going to have to pay for my past sins?"

৯

My perspective on God during this season of life was very skewed and shrouded in pain. I would blame God for everything and nothing, oscillating between the extremes of doubting his existence altogether and believing he was some kind of celestial sadist, getting a thrill out of punishing me for my past behaviors. Like the bully burning ants with his magnifying glass in the sunshine, God (if he was even real) seemed to find pleasure in causing me pain.

Deep down, I truly wanted to believe he was real and that he had helped with my job and my daughter. I wasn't comfortable living in a world without God's existence, but how could I live in one where he seemed to hate me?

These questions, while painful and difficult to reconcile, were preparing my young heart to be open and ready when God decided to reveal himself.

6

An Open Heart

*I am grateful for not having known in advance
what God was planning for me.
But I am grateful as well for the new place
that has been opened in me
through all the inner pain.*

—Henri J. M. Nouwen,
The Return of the Prodigal Son

What transpires in a person's life that finally opens their heart to the truth about God is a profound mystery, known only by the Creator himself. He alone can peer into the depths of a soul and know what it will ultimately take to open their heart to his love. While he doesn't cause the brokenness and pain they experience, he can and will use it to draw them closer to himself if they let him.

Consequences from my choices, mingled with my inadequate knowledge of the character of God, had left me feeling alone and punished for the brokenness of my past. I was lost and desperately in need of something or someone to save me from the despair that surrounded me. With no way to save myself and nowhere to turn, my heart was finally open in a way it had never been before to the things of God.

Quietly, but powerfully, he would move in, declaring, "I am here."

સ

Life moved forward with plans of building a new home now at the forefront of my thoughts. There was no longer a desire in me to try for another child as I was certain I could not go through another miscarriage alone, and Todd didn't seem to mind. So I focused on what I could control, picking flooring and paint for the new house while preparing our current home for sale. It was not glamorous, but it kept me busy and my mind away from the existential questions about God that had previously been plaguing me.

Plans and prep for our home to go up for sale were in full swing, and I was regularly in cleaning and decluttering mode. Todd was working a lot, and most of my days at home were me and our daughter Sydney hanging out together as I worked around the house. She was around two years of age, maybe a little younger and so much fun, definitely bringing a joy to my life that had previously been missing. Her favorite thing to do at that age was playing hide-and-seek, and it was not uncommon for her to disappear throughout the day. The faint sound of little giggles could regularly be heard coming from behind a curtain or under a bed initiating the game to come find her in hiding.

One day in particular, as I was cleaning, I noticed that Sydney was missing. I hadn't been alerted by her giggles but assumed from past behavior that her absence was inviting me to a game of hide-and-seek. I stopped what I was doing and through the main level of the house I went, calling out in a playful tone, "Syyyydneyyyy, wherrrre are you? Momma's gonna find you and get you. I know you're in here." Surprisingly, no giggles came and no Sydney was found. *Hmmm, where could she be?* I wondered as I walked from her bedroom back into the living room area.

Our home at the time was a split level, and Sydney was never allowed on the lower level by herself, so I was fairly certain she wouldn't be there. However, I looked across the room and noticed I had left the baby gate at the top of the stairs open as I was bringing things into the storage area on the lower level earlier in the day. Maybe she had made her way down there? Quickly, I darted down the stairs, my heart racing a bit at this point, but still remaining calm as I once again called out, "Hey little Syd, where are you? Momma's gonna find you." Once again, no giggles came. I searched the living area and then went to the storage area, but still, no Syd and my heart began to race faster.

Up the stairs I bounded and quickly went through the living room, bathrooms, and bedrooms on the main level once again, continuing to call out for Syd, but there was no sign of her anywhere. My momma's heart began to panic at this point and I wondered if somehow she had gotten outside, so I rushed down the steps and out into the front yard. We lived on the corner of a very busy street, and I feared maybe she had wandered out in the road, but there was no sign of her anywhere. Immediately, I ran to the backyard looking in the shed, under the lid of the sandbox, everywhere—still, no Syd.

Terror began to sink in as I ran back into the house. Standing in the living room, I was desperately trying to decide what I needed to do next when the following thought flooded over me like a wave of despair, out of nowhere...

"What if everything I learned growing up in church was true? What if all that talk about Jesus and his returning for his people someday was real? What if he came back today, took his people and Syd because she is innocent, and left me because I am such an awful person?"

Tears filled my eyes as I stood paralyzed by these questions, for what seemed like forever, when suddenly out of nowhere, Sydney came running down the hall, laughing hysterically. Relieved, I scooped her up in my arms, whispering, "You little stinker, where have you been? Momma was so worried!" I pulled her close to my chest and enveloped her in the biggest momma hug I could give, and this is the moment God used to grab me.

As I stood there holding my little girl close, swaying side to side as mommas do, with my eyes closed, God whispered so silently but clearly into the depths of my soul, "Steph, I'm here and I'm real, and you need to get it together." The words I heard (not audibly but in my innermost being) were not harsh, condemning, or mean, but simply a statement of fact into my soul from the God I had so long doubted existed or loved me.

God had used the day's events and my past knowledge to finally grab my attention. In that brief moment, through his tender words, all doubt was immediately extinguished about his existence. God was real, which I was pretty sure meant so was his son, Jesus. The question that arose in me next was simple, "Now what?" It was great to finally feel confident in God's existence, but shouldn't this only affirm my lingering thoughts about him hating me and punishing me for my past? I wasn't so sure. The words whispered into my soul were not condemning but inviting and I wondered for the first time since I was twelve, "Maybe God does love me?"

ॐ

"Now what?"

This question lingered in my young, open heart and mind for weeks after that day, but I honestly had no idea what I should do next. Was going back to church the answer? I wasn't so sure, but it was the only thing I knew to do at the time, so I decided to start there.

What a mess this endeavor proved to be! Initially, Todd had no interest at all in going with me, though he said he would be supportive of my checking things out, so I would go by myself. I had no concept of denominations or theological perspectives, so I simply chose churches that were close to my house. Most were just boring with seemingly no application to life today and others were just plain odd. Of course, the one Sunday I was able to convince Todd to check out a church with me, we landed in a weird one.

Driving into the parking lot, everything seemed normal. The people didn't dress weird and everyone appeared friendly and genuinely happy to be there. It was a larger church and had a school associated with it, so I was optimistic. Worship was good, though Todd and I were not into the singing so we just stood there listening. I remember looking around at the people, wondering, *Do they really believe what they are singing? I'd be curious to know if they actually mean it?* Finally, after three songs and a few announcements, we sat down to hear the message.

The topic was "giving," and I was so disappointed. I had finally gotten Todd to agree to come to a church, and all he was going to hear about was how people should give to the church. If God was watching all of this play out, he certainly had a twisted way of trying to draw us closer. I remember thinking, *Why would God let me bring Todd on a day like this?* I knew this was not going to end well, but I remained hopeful. Unfortunately, my hopes were immediately dashed as the message quickly turned from the topic of giving to *radical* giving.

As the pastor expounded on the benefits to your soul when you give to God, he made an outrageous request to the congregation. Quite seriously, he asked, "For the next nine months, would you be willing to give your 10 percent to the church joyfully and obediently, while saving as much as you can? Then in the last three months of the year, would you be willing to give your entire salary to the church?" I felt like all the air left my body, and I could barely breathe. As I glanced over at Todd, his face was beginning to redden with anger, so I quickly grabbed his hand as I saw him starting to rise. Looking squarely into his eyes, I whispered, "It's okay, let's finish this, and then we'll go."

When the last song came to a close, Todd bolted out of the sanctuary like his hair was on fire. I quickly went to the nursery to grab Sydney and then met him in the car. His words were clear and final, "I am *never* doing that again. All these churches are filled with hypocrites and just want your money. You can keep going, but don't ever ask me again." There was no arguing with his perspective or feelings on the matter; the issue was settled.

I was just as angered by the pastor's request and had already decided I was not going to return to this particular church, so once again, the question came, "Now what?" The churches I had been trying were clearly not connecting with my searching heart and I hated going alone. Now it was clear from Todd's declaration that I would always be going by myself. At the time, I desperately wanted to be faithful and figure out what God wanted of me, but despite my efforts, I simply did not have the strength to go it alone. After a few more months of church shopping, I gave up.

My heart, however, had been reopened to God, truly open for the first time in more than ten years. While I may have given up on the idea of church, I had not given up on the reality of God. In his grace, Jesus would keep drawing closer through every means possible and make a way for me to find him.

๑

Nothing significant happened in my faith journey, besides the church disappointment, after the day God whispered into my soul. Life just continued moving forward. We finished building our new home, moved in, and quickly found a rhythm to life. I worked, Todd worked, and my grandma drove to our home daily to watch Sydney, which was such a gift. In all truthfulness, it wasn't a bad existence, and there was a lot of good in our life. Despite our brokenness, there was love; it was simply marred by past pain that we were ignoring. It's like we were reaching for a level of happiness that was always slightly beyond our grasp, and though we couldn't pinpoint the reason why, we felt its loss.

Despite our internal restlessness, the next season of life brought the unexpected joy of another child. We had officially stopped trying for another baby, but due to migraine complications, I had to discontinue birth control and another pregnancy surprised us. I was understandably nervous for the first three months, and we shared the news with only minimal family until we felt reasonably safe that things were moving forward. Thankfully, everything about the pregnancy was without issue or complication and in September 1997, a son was added to our little family.

I remember so vividly the day Todd brought Sydney to the hospital to meet baby Cody. A good friend suggested that Cody bring a gift for Sydney when he first met her as a way to acknowledge her role as the big sister in the family. This could not have been a better idea! Sydney was three and a half at the time and entered the hospital room hesitantly, staring at me holding Cody as I sat in the bed. To break the tension, I motioned Todd toward my suitcase, while saying to Syd, "Hey, sweetie, Cody was so excited to meet you today that he brought you a present." Her eyes widened with anticipation as Todd handed her the small, wrapped gift. Quickly she removed the paper and bow revealing her favorite movie on VHS, *Pooh's Grand Adventure*. Speechless, she stood there, tears welling up in her little eyes.

While she had been opening the present, I handed Cody off to Todd to hold, and he was now sitting with him in a chair nearby. Cody's little body lay snuggly in the space between Todd's legs as his hands interlocked behind Cody's neck for support. A perfect way to gaze at his little boy while watching Sydney opening her gift in the background. Looking over at Cody, Sydney slowly placed the movie on the floor and moved toward him. My momma's heart began to melt as I watched her gently cup Cody's little head in her small hands, lean in close to his ear, and whisper, "Oh, Cody, thank you so much, it's my favorite."

Sitting there, looking at Todd with our two children, my heart was fuller than it had ever been. However we had gotten there, whatever brokenness may have been in our past, this was my family, and I was committed 100 percent to all three of them. All my selfish desires seemed to melt away in that moment, and my family was now the highest priority.

The next several years brought a surge of success and stability in both mine and Todd's careers. For a couple in our midtwenties from a small town, we were doing exceptionally well at "keeping up with Joneses" mentality our culture encourages and were materially thriving. The cost, however, was higher than my young momma's heart wanted to pay. Todd, of course, didn't seem to mind the sixty to eighty-hour work weeks, but for me, anything above the regular nine-to-five brought feelings of intense guilt.

My children were in great, loving hands during the day as my retired grandmother had taken up the job of daycare for us. It was by far the most perfect situation you could conceive. She got paid well during retirement, and we had someone who would drive to our home daily, not only to watch our children but love them from a depth of soul that only a great-grandma's love can give to her granddaughter's children. Of course, there were moments when she was being too much of a great-grandma to them, not disciplining or correcting, but overall, the love she gave far outweighed them being spoiled.

It's one thing, however, to know your children are cared for when you must work, but it is something different when you see work unnecessarily pulling you away from significant occasions with your family. While feelings of guilt plagued me on the nights I had to work late, which were often, I could not reconcile missing important traditions we had begun to establish with our children in those early years.

Coloring Easter eggs was one of our favorite traditions when the kids were little, and we made a big deal about the evening, not only getting the dye, but glitter, markers, stickers, and whatever else may stick to a hard-boiled egg. It was always a fun evening full of mess and giggles. Typically, we would color the eggs on Good Friday, which would give the kids both Saturday and Sunday to play with the eggs and dote over their fancy egg creations. For five years, this had been an established tradition, so when year 6 came along, as I was required to stay late at work to meet a deadline, I was crushed.

I remember getting the call from my grandmother that night: "Steph, honey, I'm so sorry to bother you at work, but the kids want to know when you'll be home."

Sydney's little voice was echoing in the background. "Let me talk to her." She was not upset when she got on the phone, just trusting that our tradition would happen and inquiring, "Mom, when are you gonna get here to color eggs?"

In a surprising way, Syd's voice brought a sense of clarity to the moment rather than guilt. There I was working late, missing an important tradition, for what? While the deadline was import-ant, it wasn't significant enough to miss this occasion, so I pushed things off until Monday and left for home. There would be minor consequences for the decision, but ultimately, my heart knew the consequence to my family would be far greater if I didn't choose them. So I did and never looked back.

In the months to follow, God would honor my decision to choose my family over work and open the door for a new job at a small company near my home. It was a cut in pay, but the hours were flexible, and I could be home more regularly. It was not a role that was going to bolster my career, but I didn't care. What was most important to me was my family and I finally had the ability to be present for them. Thankfully, Todd was supportive of the switch as well. Of course, I didn't recognize God's hand in this situation early on, but he would show it soon enough.

Unknown to me at the time, the couple who owned the company I switched to were Christ-followers. They were not pushy in their faith or overbearing, but they were open and forthcoming about what they believed. So when they invited me to check out their church, I was not surprised. It had been such a long time since I'd been in a church, but at least now, I would not have to go alone so I said yes.

It was such an odd feeling to be back in church the Sunday I went, and yet it felt incredibly comfortable. Upon arrival, I was pleasantly surprised by the friendliness of the greeters and even more surprised by the way the music and message drew me in to want more. I wondered as I left, "Hmmm, maybe this is what church is supposed to feel like?" I definitely was not ready to commit to anything, but my heart was open to giving it another week. The following Sunday I returned, and the week after, and the week after, and the week after. Five weeks later, I would find myself praying silently from my seat a prayer of rededication to Jesus as the service came to an end. I had no idea what lay ahead of me on my faith journey, and in many ways, I am grateful for my ignorance, but whatever was to come I was back in a relationship with Jesus for the first time in fifteen years and it felt like home.

ॐ

It's an odd phrase to use about a relationship with a God you can't see, but during this season of rekindling my faith, I was daily "falling in love with Jesus." No, I could not visibly see him or audibly hear him, but in the depths of my soul, he was continuously revealing his presence to me in profound ways by the power of his Holy Spirit. I was doing my part, soaking up everything I could find to know him better, reading every book, listening to every message on Christian radio, selectively watching TV ministries, taking classes at church, praying, learning to read the Bible for myself, and Jesus was meeting me in every step I took. It was a precious time of spiritual growth and building a relationship with Jesus, but it was also an incredibly confusing time as I lived in the tension between the two extremes of loving Jesus and loving Todd.

My relationship with Jesus was welcoming and safe while my relationship with Todd was always on edge. I tried to walk this line carefully to honor both of my loves, but the more I grew in relationship with Jesus, the more I saw his desire to have my heart above anything or any person in my life. It wasn't an unfair request when I considered all Jesus had done for me; I simply didn't know what it would be like in practicality. I knew what God's word said about the covenant of marriage, so I was certain he wasn't asking me to leave Todd, even if he didn't believe the same as me. But how could I live fully for Jesus in a relationship with someone who didn't believe as I did and who was becoming increasingly hostile toward my attempts at spiritual growth?

There were no easy answers or quick fixes to my questions. In fact, what I continued to experience was a daily decline in my marriage the closer my relationship with Jesus became. How could this be? My thoughts arrested me as I pondered, "If I was willing to set aside my old life and finally walk faithfully with Jesus, why weren't things getting better in my marriage? Surely, God was going to intervene at some point, but when and how? And if he didn't, what was going to happen to us?" I struggled greatly with these questions, but despite the silence from God when I asked them, I kept moving forward. The reality of Jesus had become clear to me and there was now no turning back, so I kept hoping for a miracle.

୨

Hope. It's one of those words, in the natural realm, that for many people oscillates between delusion and positive thinking. In the spiritual realm, however, it means something quite different. Hope is the ability to trust God in situations that seem bleak and hopeless. It's the one word that beacons us from the throne of God's eternal glory to believe he can and will do whatever is necessary to cradle our hearts with his love in the most unimaginable moments of pain and confusion.

Was I delusional for thinking God might be able to fix my marriage or was I living in Christian hope? Some days, I honestly could not tell.

This season was brutally disappointing as Todd pulled further and further away from me and our children. Hostility arose weekly as I continued to take the kids to church amidst Todd's protests, and then the events of 9-11 hit, propelling his heart and mind into profound confusion. Wave after wave of deep despair seemed to continuously crash over him while I sat back, helplessly, watching him drown in his own sea of hopelessness. He coped by distancing himself from us in his rehab project and working, even more, leaving me feeling more isolated than ever.

This is the season God led me to the *Focus on the Family* radio show and the story of the woman who had been assaulted, as well as the book of Job. While I didn't understand and struggled to get my mind around the levels of surrender Job and the woman had with God in their devastating stories, the timing could not have been more perfect. God knew, at the time, my heart was open to receiving his message of hope through these very different lives and stories. He also knew, though I was wrestling and pushing hard against what I heard, I would need the lessons in these stories of surrender to be ready for what was coming.

The wall of objections I put up against this kind of love and surrender to God was thick and tall. I did love him, but "I could never love him like that," not in a way that allowed him to seemingly abandon me to the brutality and loss I saw in Job and the woman's stories. It all felt a bit maddening. I had come so far in my relationship with Jesus and now I sat saying, "Nope, no further." Rationally, it all made sense (no one willing signs up for pain), but something deep inside me kept pulling me closer and closer to God through the questions and wrestling. In the end, I concluded, either these people were, in fact, delusional, *or* God truly did transform them in their darkest hours, giving them strength and resilience through crushing sorrow. If the latter was true, would he do that for me?

I rationalized for weeks how it might happen if God chose to intervene but, of course, came up empty. The only thought I kept coming back to was, "Surely it can't get as bad as Job." So in desperation, I took the step that would forever change the course of my existence, and I surrendered my family.

I remember that moment today like I am still in the room. It was early on Monday morning, 5:00 a.m. to be exact, and I was at the office. The building was completely silent as no one else was due to arrive until about 7:00 a.m. I liked to come in early on Mondays for time alone with God before the pressures of the week began. I had just finished my Bible reading for the day and was reflecting on the disparity between what I read about and what my life actually looked like. How was God ever going to fix it? The woman from *Focus on the Family* popped into my head and the thought came, "God helped her." I sat for a long time, my mind lingering in her story, when thoughts of Job's story intruded and I realized, "God helped him too."

Slowly, I rose from my chair and walked around to the front left corner of my desk, placing my hand on it to steady myself as I looked at the carpet in front of me. Was I really going to do this? Yes, because at that moment, what I knew to be true was that God was the only answer to my problem. Gently, I slid down to the floor and sat, knees in front of me with my bottom on my heels and hands on my thighs. Leaning forward, one by one, I placed my hands on the floor in front of me and then gradually lowered my head until my forehead rested on the carpet. Tears flooded my eyes and my nose began to run as I prayed, "Okay, Lord, whatever you have to do to save my family, do it."

The prayer was simple, and in the span of five seconds, I had given God permission to do "whatever" he wanted to save my family. Was I ready for what would come next? Simply put, no.

I have always been someone who finds comfort in thinking through everything that can possibly go wrong in the hope of preparing for it in advance. What would we do if Todd lost his job? How would we handle it if one of the kids got really sick? How will we navigate losing one of our parents someday? Morbid in some ways, but comforting to try and emotionally prepare. The problem is, none of the bad scenarios I've ever tried to prepare for have ever happened. On the contrary, almost every bad thing that has hit me was never on my radar and completely blindsided me. The permission I'd given God to do "whatever" would be the same.

Three weeks after my prayer, surrendering my family to God, I lay in bed watching TV. It was almost 11:30 p.m., and Todd was still not home. He was working late at the rehab house but was supposed to be home an hour and a half ago. What was taking him so long? He knew I didn't sleep until he got home. I had to work in the morning and felt disrespected by the fact that he hadn't even checked in to let me know he was going to be later than expected.

Finally, close to midnight, I shut off the TV and decided to try and sleep. Closing my eyes, I heard the familiar sound of the garage door opening and comfortingly said to myself, "Finally, now maybe I can get some sleep." Laying there, sleep did not come as I kept waiting for Todd to come to bed. I wondered, *What is he doing? What is taking so long?* After about thirty minutes, I finally got up to see what was going on. Quietly I made my way down the hallway, careful not to wake the kids and into the living room. Through the darkness, I could see Todd sitting in the kitchen at the table.

The image of that evening is forever burned into my mind. The table was white with fake purple lilies sitting in the middle. One of my metal, stainless steel mixing bowls sat in front of Todd (still in his work clothes from the day) filled with leftover salad from the dinner he had missed with us. He wasn't eating it, though. Instead, he sat with his face over the bowl, both hands cradling his temples as he sat rocking back and forth, sobbing. Quietly, I walked over and pulled out the chair next to him to sit down. My presence was unmistakable, but still, he said nothing, so I slid both of my hands across the table and grabbed his left forearm. Without hesitation, he lowered it, and I held his hand cupped in mine. Awkwardly, we sat staring at each other, tears streaming down his face. Breaking the silence, I said, "Sweetie, what's wrong? You can tell me. Whatever it is, we'll be okay."

I remember him looking down at my hands holding his as he began fidgeting, his thumb moving back and forth, tapping inside my hand and his left foot shaking uncontrollably under the table.

"What is it?" I whispered.

Finally, he spoke, "You already know."

I questioned, "What? What do I already know?" My mind began spinning. I thought of the night a few months ago when he hadn't come home. I had confronted him, not with an affair, but with whether he wanted to be married anymore. At the time, my mind simply would not allow itself to conceive this to even be a possibility, but now here I sat, Todd looking me in the eyes, confirming what my heart knew but my mind would not allow me to see.

I could barely hear him but the words were unmistakable, "I've been having an affair."

I said nothing, simply staring at him in disbelief until the words formed, "With who?"

He cocked his head to the right in a manner that said, "You know," and my heart immediately sunk into my stomach. Quickly,

I snatched my hands away from his in disgust. I had been right. All my inner uncomfortableness with this coworker of his had been spot on. How had I been so stupid? She had even bought Girl Scout cookies from my daughter. Leaning forward, I clenched my stomach, wanting to vomit as torrents of tears rushed into my eyes.

I got up to walk away, but Todd would not let me. Calmly, he whispered, pushing the tears from his eyes, "We need to talk about this."

Angrily I retorted, "Okay, fine, yeah, let's talk about this?" I spewed all sorts of ugly angry things at him. and he surprisingly took it until the conversation came near to a close. I was done yelling and simply, quietly, and without anger said, "I just don't understand. How could you do this? How could you stand before God, our family, and all our friends, committing to be faithful to me and our marriage and do this?"

As I stood looking at him waiting for a response, I watched as his countenance visibly changed. He stood straight up and with a scowl said, "Huh, isn't that a good question when you did the exact same thing to me!"

I demanded, "What are you talking about? I've been faithful to you our entire marriage!"

Shaking his head, he backed away from me as he spoke, "No. When we were dating, I loved you and was committed to you like you were my wife and you betrayed me. You did the exact same thing, and now we're even." With that, he moved toward the hallway and said without emotion, "I have to work in the morning. This conversation is over. I'll sleep on the couch."

Todd's pain had finally exploded all over our life, and God had allowed it.

෨

That night so long ago, felt like the equivalent of God placing his divine heel on us, slowly, intentionally, crushing us under his weight, in swift back and forth motions. I had dared to hope for a miracle, and this is what came? It seemed like just as much a betrayal by God as it did by Todd. Whatever had transpired to this point, one thing was for certain: the pulverization was complete, and everything in my marriage was completely broken.

Prior to this event, my heart had slowly been reopened to Jesus, and he knew I was now ready to experience what the power of complete surrender to God could accomplish. The question was, "Would I be able to do it?"

Part 2

EVERYTHING SURRENDERED

Come to me, all you who are weary and burdened,
and I will give you rest.

—*Matthew 11:28 (NIV)*

Trust in the Lord with all your heart
and lean not on your own understanding;
in all your ways submit to him,
and he will make your paths straight.

—*Proverbs 3:5–6 (NIV)*

7

The Choice

*So we will be brought one by one to the testing
place, and we may never know when
we are there. At that testing place there will
be no dozen possible choices for us—
just one and an alternative—
but our whole future will be conditioned
by the choice we make.*

—A. W. Tozer,
The Pursuit of God

*Free will and the ability to make choices is one of the most powerful gifts
God has given to mankind. The capacity to think, act, and choose is a
beautiful manifestation of our being created in His image and carries with
it much responsibility. The problem, however, is free will was given to all
people, which means there will be those who will make choices that bless
others and those who will make choices that harm others. In my humanness,
I wish God would have only given this gift to those who choose wisely, but
that's not how it works. It's an everyone or no-one gift, undergirded with the
promise that God can bring good out of any situation (Rom. 8:28 NIV).
Even the most unspeakable evil and unbearable pain brought about by
man's brokenness can be redeemed by God, but this, too, requires a choice.
Will we use our free will to believe God can redeem and trust the path he
takes us down to do so? Or will we remain in our pain, victimized by the*

choices of others? God's gift of free will allows us to choose, and that choice will forever define the rest of our lives.

In the midst of my most life-shattering pain, God was about to set before me a choice that would forever change the trajectory of my life. My choice would not make sense to many people, but it would be the decision that changed my entire future and started my journey toward surrendering everything to God.

The six hours following Todd's confession of infidelity were brutal. He had grabbed his pillow and headed to the couch to sleep, leaving me alone in our bedroom to process everything that had just transpired. No sleep came as I spent my time sobbing hysterically in the bed or racing to the bathroom to vomit. By morning, I was utterly exhausted. My face was red and puffy, my eyes were horribly swollen, and my back hurt from the last two hours of dry-heaving with nothing left in me to expel. Around 5:30 a.m., I heard Todd moving around, preparing to leave for work just as he'd declared the night before. No words were exchanged between us as he dressed and swiftly left.

Standing there all alone in the bathroom, my head began spinning as the thought rushed in, and the tears once again began to flow: *What am I supposed to do?*

At that moment, I felt like I had nowhere to turn. I had pulled away from many of my non-Christian friends because I was still figuring out my faith and didn't know how to do life with them. But I hadn't made any new Christian friends because I didn't want to explain why my husband didn't come to church or share how broken my past had been. Additionally, I knew that because both my mom and grandmother had been betrayed by their spouses, they would simply counsel me to leave Todd. Maybe that's what I should do, but in my current state of shock, I wasn't ready to make that decision.

As I tried to figure out my next steps, I was thankful the kids were still sleeping. Grandma, however, would be arriving any minute to watch them so I could head off to work. Clearly, I was a mess; what was I supposed to tell her? I hurried to my bedroom door and locked it. Grandma had a key to get in the house and would most likely start tidying the kitchen and get coffee ready for me, so I felt somewhat safe. My heart pounded as I heard her enter and walk down the hallway to lightly tap on my bedroom door, "Stephy, you up?"

I took a deep breath, steadied my voice, and said, "Uh, yeah, I just overslept and I'm jumping in the shower. Having some trouble with allergies today so gonna see if I can get into the doctor this morning." I hated lying to her, but I didn't know what else to do.

"Okay," she cheerfully replied, "I'll get Syd moving for school and have coffee ready soon."

Dropping my head, more tears came as I clenched my throat, mustering a faint, "Thanks."

The kids soon began moving about, so I went into the master bathroom, locked the door, and turned on the shower. It would be the only safe place to fully express my pain without fear of being seen. Opening the glass shower door, I stepped inside and looked back out through the steamy glass, across the sink into the mirror. The question came, "Who is that pathetic woman looking back at me?" With this, I sunk naked into the basin of the shower, clasped my arms around my legs, buried my head in my knees, and sobbed uncontrollably for fifteen to twenty minutes as the water flowed over me masking my loud sobs.

Finally, I was able to pull myself up, dressed, and emerged from the bedroom looking pretty rough. I'd already called my boss and told him I wasn't coming in because of the "allergy" issue, and now I would have to face Grandma. It only took a brief look for her concern to pour out, "Oh my goodness, honey, what happened to your face?"

I mustered a smile and once again lied, "It's some sort of allergic reaction. I'm actually heading to the doctor right now." With that, I kissed my kiddos, grabbed my purse, and headed out the door with absolutely no idea where I was going.

ॐ

Approaching the stop sign at the exit to our subdivision, panic began to set in, and my hands began to shake as I pondered the simple decision in front of me. Right or left? Tears began to flow as I wondered, "Where am I supposed to go?" Looking to the right, I saw the Burger King that I'd so many times visited with my kids. For now, this would have to be my resting spot as I figured out what to do next. There was no way I could go inside and be around people, so I pulled through the drive-through, got a large coffee, and parked.

Once settled, the first thing I did was call my church, hoping maybe my pastor could give me some wisdom on how to proceed. To my surprise, he was unavailable for the entire week. Knowing I was about to emotionally go under, I shared briefly what had happened and pleaded with the receptionist to direct me to anyone else on staff or in the congregation who might be able to talk with me. Her words were emotionless, "I'm sorry, he can see you next week, could you meet on Monday?" Immediately, my heart felt the familiar sting of God's church and his people once again disappointing me. This time, however, I was not about to let people ruin God for me, so I set the appointment and hung up.

Up to this point, I had not been able to bring myself to pray. The pain in my chest was so intense that it literally felt like my heart was broken, and all I knew was that God had allowed it. After all my changes, all my attempts at growth, and my final desperate plea for God to save my family, this is what he had brought. I simply had no words for him. It was an odd dichotomy, knowing that I needed God but also feeling so incredibly mad and disappointed by him.

More than four hours passed as I sat in the Burger King parking lot, feeling utterly alone. The first two hours were me hunched over the steering wheel oscillating between fits of sobbing rage and confused despair. Eventually, though, the tears stopped and despite all my anger and disappointment, I knew in the depths of my soul there was only one person I could turn to for help. It was not eloquent or even faith-filled, but I was finally able to muster these four words in a prayer of desperation, "Jesus, help me, please."

I can't fully explain what happened next, except to say that in the next few hours, Jesus brought a strength and a perspective that I needed to help me figure out what to do.

Perspective came as he reminded me of all I'd been learning about his character over the past year. My current situation had not changed what I knew about Jesus. In spite of everything I was feeling, I knew he loved me and I could trust that I was not alone in that parking lot. He was sitting there in that SUV, weeping right alongside me, just as heartbroken as I was over all that had happened. But even though he wept with me, I was also reminded of his sovereignty and that he was not surprised or caught off guard by what happened. While he had not caused it, Todd's free will was to blame, all the events that transpired were filtered through his hand and he could bring something good out of it, if I would allow him.

Oddly enough, this perspective gave me the strength I needed to pick up the phone and make two phone calls. The first was to Todd, telling him he needed to meet me at his parents' house, who were out of town, to discuss what was going to happen with our marriage. I was not emotional or demanding, but strong and direct in such a way that he did not hesitate to comply. The second was to the woman with whom he'd had the affair. Again, I was not mean or ugly, but I was direct, stating that I knew about the affair and that it was now over. At first, she tried to deny it, but the strength Jesus gave me would not allow it, and she eventually admitted everything. I didn't feel happy about the admission but was glad I stood up for myself in a way that honored my Savior. This, in and of itself, was a miracle.

The "high" of standing up for myself quickly wore off, though, and I was once again left with the knowledge that my marriage and family were crumbling. However fully I wanted to cling to hope at this moment, I could not see any good coming from what was happening to us. Now that Todd was coming to talk about things, what in the world was I going to say? Were we over? I honestly had no idea, and once again, the pain in my chest returned with sharp stabs, along with the tears.

§

Sitting across from Todd, out on the sun porch at the back of his parents' house, it was clear he had no idea he was about to lose everything. For almost an hour, we had talked about the past and how we had ended up in our current state of relational brokenness. While Todd sincerely expressed his sadness and remorse over what he had done and declared in no uncertain terms that the affair was over, he didn't seem to realize the deep fracture this caused in our marriage. In his mind, we were now "even" in the pain we'd caused one another and should be able to just move on. The problem was, I couldn't live in a marriage like that, always weighing one another's brokenness, waiting for opportunities to pay each other back. Plus, this was no longer just about us. We had two beautiful children who would grow and model what we would show them about relationships, love, and God. How could I stay in this marriage with his mindset?

No conclusion would come from our talk except we would keep the affair hidden until we could figure out what to do. In the meantime, we would pretend like life was okay in front of our kids, friends, and family. Daily we would both put on a fake smile and go about life. At night, we would tuck the kids into bed and then go into our bedroom as normal to give them the illusion of our togetherness, then when they'd fallen asleep one of us would head to the couch.

The problem with our decision was it was getting harder for me to hide my despair. By nature, I'm an overthinker, so daily my mind was racing through a million questions about what had happened, wanting details and things that are not helpful for healing from a betrayal. Still, I wanted answers. Additionally, I was not sleeping because when I would close my eyes, all I could see was Todd and this woman together, so nightly I'd stay up watching TV until

I passed out, leaving me exhausted. Then there was my inability to eat. The whole situation left me so disgusted that I couldn't eat anything, losing 7–10 lbs. that first week. The exhaustion, the weight loss, and the look of stress on me were bringing about questions from family, and we needed to figure out what to do soon.

God wasn't saying much the week following my time with him at Burger King, and once again, I had little to pray beyond "help," so I decided to call an old friend and get away for the weekend to figure out my thoughts. She had access to a condo in the Lake of the Ozarks, Missouri, and had family there to visit, so it was a win for both of us. Maybe God would speak there?

♀

It's funny how quickly our old nature can move back in on us. Regardless of how faithful we try to remain to God, it's always there, waiting to emerge, once again leaving us with a choice to return to what is familiar or cling to God. As hard as I was trying to cling, my grip was weakening.

My arrival at the Lake of the Ozarks was on St. Patrick's Day weekend, and the town was in full swing of party mode. My initial intent was time away to think and figure things out, but my old nature whispered, "Screw it! Let's go get wasted and maybe even find someone to get back at Todd with for what he's done." It's shameful to even admit that this was my thought. However, regardless of what my flesh whispered, my heart was different. Instead of doing something stupid that would further destroy my marriage (if that was even possible), I would spend the entire weekend in prayer.

Now, I will not pretend that this was some super-spiritual, bathed-in-God retreat. My heart was broken, and there was drinking as I so desperately wanted to numb myself from the pain. But quite often, what was transpiring was me sitting in the hot tub alone with a beer pouring out my pain to God. Me burying my head in a pillow, screaming through sobs for God to please help and stop the pain in my chest. Or me on the phone screaming at Todd about what he'd done because alcohol had given me a bravery to say things that I might not otherwise have said. Am I proud that I leaned back on this old crutch of alcohol? Of course not, but in hindsight, it reveals a life in process with Jesus. Sometimes, he delivers us from afflictions for them never to return. Other times, he brings healing along the way, which is how he worked in my story.

 confined

The two-and-a-half-hour drive back home from the lake was eerily silent, except for the one understandable question from my friend, "What are you gonna do, Steph?"

Staring out the window, I simply shook my head. "I have no idea. I love Todd, but I don't think we can survive this." Then the return to silence as I continued to stare out the window, overcome with dread as each mile marker revealed my return to our broken family.

Oddly enough, though I had poured my heart out to God all weekend with no answers, it was during the silence of the drive back that clarity finally came. I remember the "aha moment" of thinking, "Oh, now I get it. This would not have been the way I would have chosen it, but God has given me a biblical way out of this marriage. Now I am free to leave, and who knows, maybe God has a Christian man in my future who will love me well and help me raise my children in a Christian home. This would definitely not have been my plan, but if this is God's plan, I will try and trust him in it."

Maybe it was because I was emotionally, mentally, physically, and spiritually exhausted by this point, but the realization of God's plan brought little emotion. An answer had finally come, and I would move forward. So with that, I picked up my cell phone, called Todd, and asked him to meet me at our house without the children in about an hour. The plan was to tell him I was done and to ask him to pack up his stuff and leave. While I wasn't sure how all the details would flesh out, I knew I would keep the house and raise the kids there. Todd loved his kids, so I was certain he would support his children. It would not be easy, of that I had no illusions, but it was the path I was willing to take.

≫

Pulling into the driveway, I was surprisingly calm for someone whose world was about to completely unravel. Maybe it was blissful ignorance about how hard life was about to become. Or maybe it was trusting God's plan. Most likely it was a little of both. Regardless, there was no turning back. The garage door was up, and I could see that Todd was home.

"Do you want me to come in with you?" my friend asked.

"No, I've got this. Thanks for the weekend. I really appreciate it." And with that, I gave a half-hearted smile and got out of the car.

Walking into the house through the garage, I dropped my suitcase in the laundry room before entering the kitchen. There was no sign of Todd as I made my way through to the living room, but something odd caught my eye. There by the recliner was a stack of books about a foot tall. I couldn't make out the exact titles, but I could see words like *God* and *Jesus* on the spines. Immediately, my heart went into a rage, thinking, *I don't know why these are here, but whatever the reason, I don't care. It's too little, too late.* Todd's not a big reader, and if this was some last-ditch attempt to connect with me, I was not having it. I simply passed the chair with a head shake of disgust and made my way to the hallway leading to the bedroom. "I'm here," I yelled and then went to sit on the couch.

Sitting there on the couch waiting for him, I could feel my heart hardening within my chest. In all truthfulness, I needed it that way to find the strength I would need to tell him to leave. Slowly, from the back of the house, he emerged and walked toward me.

"Can I sit here next to you?" he asked.

"Sure, whatever," I retorted as I scooted further away from him to the middle of the couch. From this point on in the conversation, I honestly don't remember much. It felt like a scene from Charlie Brown where his teacher is speaking, "Wah wah woh wah wah." I don't remember what he said because, honestly, I didn't care.

All I was doing was waiting for a break in the conversation when it would be appropriate for me to tell him to pack his things and leave.

Roughly an hour passed when, finally, the conversation drew to a close. There was nothing left to say, and as we sat there staring at each other for what felt like forever, I finally mustered up the courage to speak and tell him to leave. I looked down at my hands, ringing them together as I tried to calm my nerves and gather my thoughts. My heart felt like it was going to pound right out of my chest, but eventually, I looked up at him, ready to speak. I opened my mouth, but before the words came out, Todd whispered, "Can I ask you one last question?"

Shrugging my shoulders and grimacing, a little irritated that I'd been interrupted, I said, "Sure, why not?"

With a very forlorn look on his face, he furrowed his brow and asked with deep sincerity, "Steph, if your God is real and he loves you the way you say he does, why did he let me hurt you like this?"

Tears filled my eyes as I absorbed his words, searching for an answer. The truth is, though I wouldn't have verbalized it that way, I had the same thoughts deep down. What was I supposed to say? Like the speed of light, my mind scanned its mental database of all the things I'd learned about God in the past year. Did he really love me? Did I truly believe he would never abandon me and that he could be trusted in any situation? Would God really allow me to suffer this way if he truly loved me? A million thoughts and questions flooded my mind in the span of thirty seconds as I desperately tried to form a response.

Then it happened, the moment that would change everything. Deep into the recesses of my soul, so very tenderly, my Savior whispered, setting before me a question. His words were clear and unmistakable, not harsh or demanding but rather like an invitation from a dear friend, "Steph, would you stay and show him I'm real?"

The tears now began to slowly stream down both sides of my face as I pondered the choice set before me. Only months before, I had begged God to intervene, to save my family, and now he was speaking so very clearly. The words were not a hypothesis in my mind or a thought prompted by bad food or delusional thinking. This was most definitely not the scenario that I had imagined for this day. I had a plan that made sense but God seemed to be overriding it. I rationally concluded, "If I truly believe that the Creator of the universe is speaking to me, asking me to stay, to surrender my life in this way, am I going to say no?" The answer was simple, and with that, I looked at Todd and spoke, "I'll stay and show you he is real and that he loves me and that he loves you. But you have to go to counseling with me."

∾

When I share this part of our story, I am aware that it sounds dramatically beautiful and holy. However, there are three significant points that I beckon you to consider for the sake of clarity and honor to God. First, God is not a sadist, and he was not asking me to stay in a situation that was in any way abusive or harmful to me or my children. It was clear at this point that Todd was no longer engaged in the affair or in activities that were a further violation of our marriage covenant. Second, though I struggled to trust it, there were tangible signs of repentance and remorse in Todd for what he had done. He was not downplaying the affair or wanting to sweep it under the rug; he was owning it fully. Thirdly, moving forward was tediously slow and painful, requiring wisdom, support, and counseling from a professional. This was a crucial aspect in making sure I was not self-deceiving or justifying staying in an unhealthy relationship in the name of Jesus.

An outsider may be tempted to think God's healing in this situation was immediate, painless, and a simple choice to save my family; however, this was not the case. Jesus whispering to me that day, asking me to stay with Todd, was not a choice about whether to stay in my marriage; the choice was whether or not I would trust God's plan for whatever came next.

Mentally, I tether this choice to the story from Daniel 3, when the three young Hebrew men, Shadrach, Meshach, and Abednego were faced with the choice to bow down to a wicked king or be thrown into a fiery furnace. These young men rationalized that God could save them, "but even if he does not" (Dan. 3:18 NIV), they would not bow down to an idolatrous king. Ultimately, Jesus walked with them in the flames, and they came out unbound and unharmed. Beautiful, but was it realistic?

This was the real choice set before me. And so, with a trembling hand, I mentally grasped Jesus's and stepped into the furnace of pain, healing, and redemption with him. What he would do next, I could not comprehend. Maybe I would be engulfed by the flames of pain, destroyed by this affair, and Jesus would somehow sustain me in it. Or maybe, just maybe, he really did want me to show Todd he was real and had plans I couldn't yet see.

Whatever the outcome, I had said yes that day, and the real work of surrender began.

8

So Much Anger

Our anger can be a measure of our faith.
Believers argue with God; skeptics
argue with each other.

—Eugene H. Peterson,
Run with the Horses

Anger. As a counselor, I can give you the definition and remind you that it is always a secondary emotion, revealing underlying sadness, disappointment, pain, fear, etc. It is the tip of the iceberg sticking out of the water that we can see, a tangible way to express that which we cannot fully articulate or process with words. Clinically, this makes sense. Personally, it offers little help unless we are willing to dive deep below the surface into the frigid waters of hurt and pain to deal with underlying emotions from which the anger rises.

The request God had made of me to stay with Todd was impossible. In my own strength, I was clearly not capable of offering Todd the kind of forgiveness that would be necessary to show him God's love. While I was willing to try, the anger that daily invaded my soul beckoned to be acknowledged and validated, hijacking my ability to heal. I could not see past the pain and argued regularly with God to help me. I desperately wanted him to just take it, to help me forget, and to give me a willingness to move forward.

God, however, had something different in mind. He would help me navigate what came next, but not by magically making everything okay. No, yet another choice was set before me, another level of surrender.

Could I give my anger to God and allow him to heal it?

ॐ

The day finally arrived when Todd and I found ourselves sitting across the large desk that formed the barrier between us and my pastor, Larry. He was a kind man, offering to counsel us as a couple and then individually, as needed, for free, as we attempted to find healing for our marriage. He was a very "theological" kind of pastor who always wore a suit and tie, even if you ran into him on a Saturday morning, and who always appeared very serious, so I was skeptical if Todd would connect well with him. Regardless of my apprehension, Todd was willing, and so there we sat.

The first meeting was mostly a recap of everything that had transpired over the past month and how we were holding up in the midst of it. Pastor Larry listened intently, saying very little, but engaging with head nods and body language that let us know he was following the story and willing to stay with us in our pain. Apparently, he was not afraid of our brokenness and gave no indication of judgment, which made us feel safe.

When the session came to a close, we set our next appointment, and he set an individual time to meet with Todd as well. Rising to leave, he asked if he could speak with me alone for a few minutes. Todd obliged and headed to the door as I sat back down awkwardly, wondering what was coming. "I wanted to give you a book that I think will be helpful in your healing," he said as he perused his bookshelf. Grabbing it, he handed it to me and then sat back down.

"Thank you," I said as I quickly glanced at the title, *Torn Asunder.* I sarcastically chuckled inside, *Yep, that's about right.*

Maybe it was the look on my face or maybe just intuition but he looked warmly at me and said, "Steph, you can heal from this. And if God gets a hold of Todd's heart, not only will he save your marriage, but you may just get the husband you've always dreamed of."

I could feel the hardness once again entering my chest, coming to protect my already broken heart. My response was unintentionally cold and ungrateful, "Well, I'd just settle for God keeping him out of hell, but thank you for your encouragement." Holding the book up in my right hand, I gave it a shake and said, "I'll give reading this a shot," and rose to leave.

My naïve heart had hoped a miracle would come in that first session, but to my discouragement, I left in the same pain and anger.

We had finally shared with Todd's parents about the affair out of necessity. It was impossible for us to get to the counseling sessions without a babysitter, and we needed their help. As expected, they loved their son, and while disappointed, they were not harsh with him or me. They could clearly see we were struggling and only wanted to be supportive.

On the evenings when we had counseling, we would drop the kids off and then return to have dinner with them. They did their best to make these evenings feel "normal," but this only seemed to intensify my inner anger. My life no longer felt normal, so a dinner filled with pleasantries and conversations about baseball or the kid's school felt like I was being mocked.

I remember acutely the evening they made barbecue for dinner, a family favorite. It was not uncommon for Todd to have a cold beer while eating his barbecue and was something he'd done our entire marriage. So when his dad offered him a beer with dinner that night, I should not have been surprised or irritated by it. However, this small, insignificant gesture, triggered a pain response in me that sent me spiraling in anger for days. At the moment, I said nothing, but Todd would get an earful later.

"How could your dad be so insensitive!" I yelled at Todd on the drive home. "Doesn't he know that alcohol was involved in what you did? Doesn't he even care how that makes me feel?" On and on my brain delved deeper and deeper into the abyss of anger writing a story of apathy and insensitivity about my in-laws that simply was not true. In hindsight, I so appreciate the way they tried to shelter our children from our pain in that season, but at the time, all I really wanted was someone to validate my pain and allow me to wallow in it.

ॐ

Torn Asunder is a fantastic book for those healing from an affair after the initial shock has worn off, but as a counselor, it is not something I recommend to couples immediately following the revelation of an affair. For most offended spouses, the feelings are far too raw and complicated to even begin to process the intricacies that led to the affair. This was most definitely the case for me.

As promised, I had begun reading the book the same week Pastor Larry had given it to me. At first, I was hopeful, but that quickly turned into rage when I came to the section that talked about both spouses admitting their part in the breakdown of the marriage before the affair began. According to the book, the affair was a byproduct of much bigger problems that both spouses would have to own and work through to find healing.

I was livid! In my pain, every single word was distorted, and what my brain interpreted it as saying was "Figure out what you did wrong to make your husband cheat." Internally I screamed, "No! No! No! I am not going to take responsibility for what he did! This was his choice, not mine." With that, I closed the book and threw it on the floor where it would sit until I could return it.

The following week at our individual counseling session, poor Pastor Larry would feel the blunt hit of my disdain for the book as I walked in and chucked it across his desk at him, vehemently declaring, "You can take that book and shove it! I am not taking responsibility for this." As I plopped into the chair across from him, it was clear by the look on his face that he was not used to being spoken to with such fierce anger in his church office. "I'm so sorry," I quickly apologize, "the book wants me to say that this is all my fault and I just can't do that." To my surprise, kindness and a bit of humor filled his face as he said, "Oooo-kaaay, definitely not a good book for where you are right now. No problem, how are you today?"

His calming presence quickly disarmed the situation and we moved forward in our conversation. "Steph, how much weight have you lost?" he asked with a fair amount of concern. By this point, three or four weeks had passed, and I was down about twenty pounds.

"I'm not sure," I lied. "I just can't get myself to eat. I'm not doing it on purpose."

This part was true. I *love* food, and not eating was not by choice, I simply couldn't get anything down as my stomach was continuously in knots. "Well, if things don't improve in the next week, I think you're gonna need to see a doctor," he said with a bit of sternness.

Driving home that night, I felt like another punch had been thrown at me. Just another area in which I was failing. My mind mused, "So it's my fault the marriage fell apart and it's my fault I'm losing weight. I wonder what else is my fault I don't know about yet."

৵

Sitting in the plush, velvety green recliner we had purchased when we built our home, I gazed out the large picture window. It was a warmer than usual spring morning, and Todd was out in the front yard with the kids. I don't remember what they were playing, but I do recall clearly the huge smiles on both Sydney and Cody's faces, then ages seven and four. Around and around, they were running and giggling, absolutely aglow from the fun they were having with their dad. Todd, too, had a warm, peaceful smile on his face that I'd not seen in ages.

My heart so very much wanted to rejoice in the image I was seeing. It was a beautiful Norman Rockwell–worthy moment. This was the dad my kids so desperately needed and that I had so longed for them to have in their lives. A small smile came to my face as I thought of all my prayers, asking God to give my children this kind of father. "Thank you, Jesus," I whispered from my soul as I was aware that he was the one responsible for this moment.

Almost immediately following this moment of praise, deep sadness filled my heart and mind. Tears quickly engulfed me, blurring the glorious moment happening outside. Yes, I was so happy for my kids and for Todd, but the moment also felt so very unfair. Todd had been the one to hurt me, and I had been the one choosing to stay to save our family, but he was the one the kids were laughing with while I was inside, too depressed to go and play with them. He was the good guy, and I was the mess. None of it seemed fair.

Despite the wide range of emotions that filled my soul, I was still committed to daily being with God during this time. It was a very perplexing season as I was certain God had asked me to stay with Todd, but in my pain, I could see no way forward. All I knew to do was to keep showing up and listening for God's voice, hoping healing would come.

During this time, I found great comfort in many of the psalms of David. Reading his pleas to God gave words and expressions to my pain that I couldn't articulate but that I felt so viscerally. Through his words, I felt permission to express my anger, fear, and despair. David's words became my words and helped me to pray when my own words escaped me.

> *Do not withhold your mercy from me, O Lord;*
> *may your love and your truth always protect me.*
> *(Ps. 40:11 NIV, 1984)*

> *Listen to my prayer, O God,*
> *do not ignore my plea; hear me and answer me.*
> *My thoughts trouble me and I am distraught.*
> *(Ps. 55:1–2 NIV, 1984)*

Save us and help us with your right hand,
that those you love may be delivered.
(Ps. 60:5 NIV, 1984)

Hear my cry, O God; listen to my prayer.
From the ends of the earth I call to you,
I call as my heart grows faint;
lead me to the rock that is higher than I.
(Ps. 61:1–2 NIV, 1984)

Find rest, O my soul, in God alone;
my hope comes from him.
He alone is my rock and my salvation;
he is my fortress, I will not be shaken.
My salvation and my honor depend on God;
he is my mighty rock, my refuge.
(Ps. 62:5–7 NIV, 1984)

Flipping through the pages of that old Bible, even now I can see the remnants of my prayers so long ago, remembering how my tears fell, saturating the thin pages, staining and crinkling them forever. It's like a memorial to my desperate grasping for God, praying over his word, every tear falling on the pages as I leaned over them praying with all my heart the words of David, desperately trying to make them my own. Oh, how I hoped God would receive them and answer me.

❧

God did answer, of course, but as usual, not in the way I would have hoped. It was during this season of confusion that he would bring me to the Scripture that would slowly lead me to the healing of my anger, eventually filling me with hope for the future, but it would be a painfully slow process. And ironically, at first, the words would insight more anger in my soul than comfort.

How I landed in the book of Romans escapes me, but there I found myself for the first time in chapter 5. To that point, I'd found encouragement and questions from the first four chapters, as Romans was pretty theologically deep for my young faith. Still, I had pressed on and there I was wading into chapter 5 when I read these words: *"Not only so, but we also rejoice in our sufferings, because we know that suffering produces perseverance; perseverance, character; and character, hope. And hope does not disappoint us, because God has poured out his love into our hearts by the Holy Spirit, whom he has given us" (Rom. 5:3–5 NIV, 1984).*

Once again, I found myself livid as I read something that was "supposed" to bring comfort to my wounded heart. A myriad of questions formed. "Is God some kind of sadist? Am I really supposed to 'rejoice' in the suffering my soul is experiencing right now? This just seems mean and stupid; how could God's word say this? If there is any truth to these words, why would God show them to me right now in my pain?"

The beauty of this moment, unknown to me at the time, was God's hand in teaching me how to wrestle with his Word. I don't believe he was angered by my questions or by my irritation about what I read. As a believer, I was not required to check my brain at the door and mindlessly believe everything I read. Instead, I was invited to draw closer and figure out who God was and what his Word really meant.

Part of me simply wanted to skip over these verses and just pretend I had not seen or read them. Unlike the *Torn Asunder* book, however, I was not willing to throw the Bible at God and tell him to shove it, so I thought it would be easier to just ignore it. The problem was, I couldn't. The words haunted me all day long, "Not only so, but we also rejoice in our sufferings." Over and over, they seemed to return anytime there was a quiet moment in my head. What was I supposed to do with this verse when it made me so angry?

I felt there was little else to lose those days, so talking with God about my anger, even anger toward his Word, was all I had. It was what I learned from David in the psalms, so if it was good enough for him, it would have to be good enough for me. Daily I would ask, "Help me to understand this because it just makes no sense to me."

Clarity continued to escape me, but finally, one day, I resolved to trust the only thing I knew to be true about God to help me—he cannot lie. I may have been woefully ignorant of much in Scripture, but this truth about God's character stuck in my brain with much veracity as I remembered the words from Hebrews 6:18 (NIV), "It is impossible for God to lie." *If* God cannot lie, I rationalized, there had to be a truth in the verses from Romans 5 that I was missing.

The only verse I had ever memorized in Scripture up to this point in my life was John 3:16. As a kid, this was what you learned at Vacation Bible School, and I could rattle it off effortlessly, even after years of absence from church without thought. I can still hear my squeaky little voice and that of other children repeating alongside the teacher: *"For God so loved the world, that he gave his only begotten Son, that whosoever believeth in him should not perish, but have everlasting life" (John 3:16 KJV).*

It's a sweet memory, but beyond this verse, I'd never felt it necessary to memorize anything in the Bible, that is until these verses in Romans captured my thoughts. I couldn't shake the feeling there was something in these verses for me, so one day I grabbed a notepad from the kitchen junk drawer. Across the top of the paper in navy blue letters were the words "To Do," and below them, I printed the following verses from Romans: *"Not only so, but we also rejoice in our sufferings, because we know that suffering produces perseverance; perseverance, character; and character, hope. And hope does not disappoint us, because God has poured out his love into our hearts by the Holy Spirit, whom he has given us" (Rom. 5:3–5 NIV, 1984).*

Daily for the next six months, I would read these words, memorizing and internalizing them. At first, I hated them, feeling they were like salt being rubbed into my wounded heart, causing stinging pain. But the more time I spent with them, the more I found myself hoping they might actually be true. Eventually, hoping they might be true, turned into believing with God's help they could be true. And finally, one day coming to see they were indeed true.

In the course of time, what started as deep hatred for these verses turned to profound hope, eventually becoming my life verses. God would use his word to not only eventually heal my anger but reveal to me the offer of being a different person, one whose character could be shaped for his glory through my suffering. And the possibility of being someone who could help soothe the pain of others through her veracious belief from Romans 5:5 (NIV, 1984) that "Hope does not disappoint."

Acknowledging and allowing myself to feel my anger, in relation to my faith, during this season of life was a necessary part of my healing process. So many times, we are told to just "give it to God" but this is to deny the deep pain that sin and brokenness cause in our world. Does God want to take our pain and anger? Of course he does! But what he also wants is our heart and our trust. To move into that sphere of deep trust in the midst of my broken heart I had to be able to talk to God about my anger and to allow him to meet me in it without fear or shame. Clearly, Eugene Peterson was right, "Our anger can be a measure of our faith."

Much more was to come in my story of surrender and healing but the words from Romans 5 would now undergird it all: "And HOPE does not disappoint." Some days, clinging to this verse would come easy, other days, not so much. Still, God did not abandon me, daily coming, asking for more and more of me.

9

Giving up Security

He is no fool who gives what he cannot
keep to gain that which he cannot lose.

—Jim Elliot,
The Journals of Jim Elliot

One of our most basic needs as human beings is security; more specifically, the need for money, a place to live, and good health. In fact, noted American psychologist Abraham Maslow calls these things "Safety Needs" and ranks them second in his "Hierarchy of Needs," right above food, sleep, and water. According to his theory, these most basic needs must be satisfied before we can focus our attention on the psychological needs for love, belonging, status, respect, or even self-esteem. While there is much veracity in Maslow's Hierarchy of Needs theory, there appears to be a very blurred line within our western culture separating the difference between a want and a need. This blur leads many to elevate an unhealthy view of security over the psychological needs of individuals, to the detriment of relationships and families.

Over the years, in the midst of our pain and brokenness, Todd and I had fallen into the trap of pursuing "stuff" to numb what we felt inside. Now that our marriage and family lay shattered before us, we would have a decision to make, fight for our relationship above all else or seek to maintain our status of material security? The answer would shock and anger those closest to us and for a time leave us completely on our own with no one but each other and God.

Turns out, God would be more than enough.

ა

Anger was still a significant struggle I was working through, but after months of counseling, glimmers of hope began to emerge, indicating that maybe we could make our marriage work. There was still much healing that needed to transpire, but we were making strides. Todd and I were once again sleeping in the same bed at night, he had cut back significantly on the amount of time he spent at work, I was finally eating again, and we were spending more time with the kids together as a family. To my surprise, Todd even attended a marriage seminar at church with me during this time, at the very least showing me he had a willingness to continue working on things. Our relationship was still very fragile and forgiveness was far off, but we were both trying.

Difficult conversations were a daily part of our routine during this time as we desperately tried to work through every issue that had brought us to this breaking point. Some moments were filled with hope, other tears and frustration, but still, we pressed on. There were a few occasions when one of us seriously questioned the other about whether we could actually make the marriage work. The specifics were so hard to sit with and the raw honesty needed from both of us felt like salt being poured into our already open wound. Most days, it felt like it would be easier to just give up, but somehow, we kept resigning ourselves to try. We had come too far to give up, and before we could call the relationship "over," we had to be sure we at least gave it our best attempt.

Two profound truths rose to the surface during this season of sorting things out. One, no one else could do the hard work of rebuilding our relationship except for us. We both had to daily show up and be willing to do the work necessary for God to meet us in the healing process. And two, marital struggles were not something we could ever run away from as they would follow us wherever we went. As these two truths began to take root, a question formed, "What if we moved and started over?" I don't remember if it was

Todd or me who verbally expressed it, but it was the spark that would set on fire the next leg of my insane journey toward trusting God with everything.

ை

"What if we moved and started over?"

Ultimately, the question stemmed from many, many, discussions regarding Todd's job and the life we had built from it. He had been at his company for almost ten years and the owners loved him, treating him much like a son. Over the years, they had groomed and molded him into a fine employee with impeccable skills in his field, providing a very generous salary. It was a job and a company no one would simply walk away from at his young age, but there we were, discussing it.

We wrestled between the tension of Todd loving his company and its owners and me struggling with him continuing to work at the same place with the woman whom he had the affair. He took every possible step to offer me accountability and make me feel comfortable, but it made life complicated. Company parties and picnics were stressful if she was there, and the job that was once a safe haven was now a point of contention for both of us. I would never ask him to give up his job, but we both wondered if staying would somehow hinder our ability to heal.

Deciding what to do was even more complex because of Todd's great respect for his employer. In his loyalty, he had no desire to work for any other company in our area, feeling it would somehow be yet another betrayal on his part. So what option was there if we both believed he couldn't stay but there was no place else to go? It felt like an impossible situation as our lifestyle required his income while our relational health was prompting him to let it go.

ை

A few weeks later, sitting together at the kitchen table, staring out the sliding glass door at the sun shining on the deck, a new question arose from Todd. "What if we went warmer?"

"What?" I asked, a bit confused.

Very matter of fact, he continued, "Hear me out. We both hate the cold weather of Missouri and love the ocean and warm weather. I don't want to work for anyone else in the area, and we can't financially survive if I don't. So what if we went warmer? We know we can't run from any of this, and ultimately, it feels like we are going through it alone anyway, so why not? Why not take the kids and start over someplace warm?"

Excitement and terror flooded over me all at the same time. "Really?" I wondered out loud.

"Why not?" he responded with a shrug of his shoulders.

For a few minutes, we just sat there, quietly pondering what he had proposed.

"I'll be right back," I blurted as I jumped up and ran to the bedroom. Quickly, I reemerged with our oversized Rand McNally Large Scale Road Atlas in hand, flipping to the illustration of the United States, spanning two pages at the beginning of the book. "Okay," I spouted with a huge grin, "where do you want to go?"

Todd smiled back, his grin widening as he stood up and peered over the map. "Well, I don't want to raise the kids on the California coast, too expensive," he said without hesitation as he pointed and swiped his finger down the state of California on the map.

To which I quickly chimed in while tapping on Florida, "Well, I don't want to raise the kids on the Florida coast, too touristy."

Our eyes quickly went to the bottom of the map. "I guess that leaves us with the Gulf coast," I said with a smile. Both of us leaned in closer and perused the southern states that bordered the Gulf of Mexico. "I think Louisiana, Alabama, and Mississippi are just a little too southern for us," I wondered out loud.

To which Todd replied, "Okay, then that leaves us with Texas." Placing my right index finger in the middle of Texas, I slowly drug it down to the bottom of the state while considering out loud,

"We'd need to live near a major city with an airport so we could easily get back to Missouri if needed. Houston or Corpus Christi?"

"I think Corpus is significantly further away, so how about Houston?" Todd replied.

"Okay then, Houston it is!" I exclaimed.

Locking eyes with me, Todd then asked, "Are we really gonna do this?"

Nodding my head slowly, I hesitantly responded, "Yeah, I think we are."

The next month was filled with a flurry of plans and a roller-coaster of emotions. In some ways, it was nice to have the distraction of talking about a potential move to distract from the pain that still filled our relationship. However, when the plans slowed down, in would rush the internal question, "Are you really going to move a thousand miles away with someone you don't trust and are not sure you can forgive?" I had no answer for myself.

In 2002, there were no smartphones and the internet was not quite what it is today, but it was a great place to take our first step toward the idea of moving. So to the computer we went, typing "Yellow Pages" in the search bar. Immediately, www.yellowpages.com popped up and from there we simply searched for companies in Houston we thought could utilize Todd's job skills. Of course, hundreds of options popped up in his field of expertise, so we printed out the first five pages of names and addresses. That week, we would send Todd's resume out to fifty-two companies in Texas, stating we were relocating soon and requesting an interview. In the next few weeks, seventeen companies would respond, so we planned a trip.

Todd's parents were gracious enough to watch the kids for a week so we could go, assuming we were getting away to further heal. I hated that we were being deceptive, but we felt it unnecessary to ruffle everyone's feathers about a move if it didn't turn out, so we kept it to ourselves. In hindsight, I'm not sure if this was the best idea, but when working through pain, it's not always easy to see how your healing process is affecting others.

Our knowledge of the Houston area was nonexistent, so the week of interviews we had planned turned out to be crazy. Houston is a massive city with many large neighboring suburb cities. It was not uncommon for Todd to have three or four interviews scheduled in a day and only make it to two because the companies ended up being so far apart, sometimes by one or two hours. No Google maps back then, just the road atlas, so it was stressful. However, most of the hiring managers were gracious, understanding our ignorance of the area. Still, it was a heavy week. Todd would go to an interview, and I'd sit out in the car with my thoughts wondering if I was crazy for even considering the move. Occasionally I'd pray, "Lord, what do I do? Am I stupid for considering this? Please show me what to do."

There was no "parting of the heavens" or whisper in my heart about what to do during this time, which was frustrating. This felt like too big of a decision to make without some form of clarity. However, what did come was a strange internal peace about living in Texas. While none of the companies Todd interviewed with that week panned out, what we both found was how much we loved Houston. The people were friendly, the weather was amazing, and it just felt welcoming during a time when we desperately needed a place of solace for our family.

Walking into our counseling session with Pastor Larry the week after we returned from Texas, I was nervous. We had decided to share with him about our idea of moving and were unsure about his response. I had already convinced myself that he was going to say this was a terrible idea. I mean, who wouldn't think this was stupid in the midst of our situation? But to our great surprise, he was incredibly supportive and affirming that this move might be just the thing we needed to truly heal as a family. His words were tender, "Who knows, maybe living in an area where you have no one will teach you both how to cling to one another and be a family? I think it's a great idea."

A sigh of relief entered my soul at his words. Pastor Larry was the only other person besides me who was talking to God about our situation, so the fact that he felt confident gave me hope. He did talk us through how hard it would be and was direct about our need to continue counseling and to find a good church once we relocated, but overall, he was incredibly affirming of our decision.

స

The months that followed were full of God moments that solidified my belief in his hand gently guiding us in the move to Texas. I may not have heard his voice inside, but circumstances were revealing his loving providence and provision. First, came the job. A few weeks after our initial visit to Houston, an employer Todd had not been able to connect with called and requested an interview. This time, he flew down by himself and all the pieces came together. It was a great company that offered all we needed to make the move. We talked on the phone and together decided he should take the offer. While there, he also found a lovely city outside of Houston as well as an apartment complex that would rent to us month to month until we could find a home. Unknowingly at the time, this was my first act of rebuilding trust as I, sight unseen, allowed Todd to pick our new city and home.

While we were excited about the job, the salary was half of what Todd currently made, so decisions had to be made. What were we willing to give up to make this work? We started with our vehicles. Todd's new job offered him a company truck, which allowed us to sell his personal truck to get rid of the payment, and we chose to sell my big SUV as well and downsize to a smaller, very affordable car. This one choice eliminated a significant financial burden. We were no longer driving fancy, but we were financially freer.

Next came our home. We lived in a desirable area in a great school district, so we were confident we could sell quickly, but we really needed a good price to give us a down payment for a home in Texas. We decided to forgo using a realtor and use an agency that handles the contracts and negotiating but otherwise leaves the seller to show, etc. It was a risky move, but one that yielded us a profit significantly higher and well above what anyone said we could get for the house.

Finally, came our "stuff." I had come to disdain everything about all the "stuff" our life had become about—fancy dishes, furniture, expensive electronics, pool table, and the elaborate play gym for the kids in the backyard. I looked at it all and only saw things that we worked harder and harder to have while neglecting our relationship and family. No longer wanting any part of it, we decided to let all this go as well, and a few weeks prior to the move, we had a garage sale selling it all. The only thing we would take besides our clothes, beds, and TV was the ugly, velvety blue couch with the gold-colored wheat on it that sat in our basement. It was our first piece of furniture from our first house, purchased at a garage sale by my mother-in-law and a reminder of our humble beginnings. After all those years of striving, this was all we wanted and needed.

I think it's important to note that God was not asking us to surrender any of these things. There is nothing wrong with having nice things and enjoying the blessings he grants to us in the financial realm. However, for us, we came to see that in this season of life, these things had only served to try and anesthetize the pain we were trying to ignore. As the blinders were lifted, we chose to no longer hide behind things but rather shed everything that would hinder us from truly being present for one another and our kids. It was a season of letting go to embrace new possibilities as a family.

While letting go of the "stuff" came fairly easy, letting go of our support system would prove to be much more difficult. Our kids were the only grandchildren of Todd's parents and were the first on my side. To say that the grandparents felt betrayed by us taking the kids and moving was an understatement. With the exception of Todd's parents, no one else knew about the affair at the time, resulting in most everyone feeling blindsided by our decision to move. A common question asked regularly by most was, "Are you really leaving us for the weather?"

Add to this also the shift for our children. For eight years, my grandmother had come to our home to watch the kids so we could work. She loved them like her own, and they loved her in a way that is indescribable. There was a bond between them that was now being severed and would require much sensitivity. Syd was eight and ready for a new adventure, but Cody was only four, and the recipient of her undivided attention as the little prince of the house and would be harder to convince.

In hindsight, I wish we had handled some of the interactions with family, friends, and the kids better; but as we were still trying to heal from our own pain, it was impossible to worry about how others felt. We did care, deeply, about how hurt all the family members felt by our decision, and yet we still knew it was the right thing—at least we hoped.

❧

The weeks moved faster than I ever would have imagined as we prepared to start a new life, in a new city, where we knew absolutely no one, and finally we were only days from the move. Everything was done. Todd had resigned from his job, the house was sold, the vehicles and "stuff" were gone, and we'd said most of our goodbyes to friends and family. There was nothing left to do but actually move.

On many occasions leading up to this point, fear and anxiety would invade my mind as I wondered, "Is this whole idea stupid?" Rationally, I could see Todd was trying and wanted to save our marriage, but I still wasn't sure if I could trust or forgive him. Then add to this the fact that we knew no one in Texas made me terrified. I was fairly certain, the only support we would possibly have had to be established in a new church family, but would Todd even be on board for that? Yes, he was going to counseling with me and had attended church a few times recently, but he definitely was not all in with the God thing. Fear began to grip me as I prayed, "Lord, did I make a mistake? Please, please protect me and my children from doing something stupid."

We were leaving early Monday morning and picking up the U-Haul truck the Saturday prior to begin loading up our life. The Friday before was a flurry of activity as we were finishing boxing things up, but Todd wanted to squeeze in one final individual counseling session with Pastor Larry before leaving. His appointment was earlier than usual so he could get back to help, but he was gone much longer than expected. I wondered what was taking so long, but to my surprise wasn't worried, comforted actually by the fact that this was Todd's idea for one last session.

Finally, I heard the door from the garage into the house open and Todd's footsteps walking across the kitchen to where I was standing in the living room taping up a box. As we walked toward me, I glanced down to see a small book in his hand. "What's that?" I asked. Holding it up, I read the words printed across the front "Baptism."

Tears filled his eyes as he spoke, "I wanted to pray the prayer with you, but I couldn't wait. I accepted Jesus into my heart with Pastor Larry today." With that, he walked over and embraced me with a hug. Tears of joy streamed down my face as I tried to absorb what he was sharing, but all I really remember is thinking, *Thank you, Jesus. Thank you, thank you. Now I am ready to move.*

Outside of God, there is an unexplainable irrationalness in our decision to move in the midst of our brokenness. It was ridiculous! In the span of less than twenty minutes, we had decided to give up everything that gave us a sense of security—Todd's job, our home, our "stuff," and the support of family and friends living close to us. It was a decision seemingly made in haste but one that revealed with immense clarity what was finally most important to us...our family above all else. It was a decision, I believe, absolutely guided by the subtle hand of God as we began to lay down our pain, anger, fear, and pride to surrender our family to him.

We left everything behind, leaving us completely empty so that God could now begin to fill us with a new life centered around him. This was not our intention when talks about moving first began, but it is a beautiful picture of how God was orchestrating things behind the scenes to draw us to himself. He knew in ways we did not, what was going to be needed to bring full healing to our marriage. Texas held the church and the people we would need to rebuild. It would be harder than we ever anticipated but worth it for what we would walk away with years later, and never once have we regretted giving up the "stuff" for what we gained.

10

Life in the Meantime

*Faith is about how you live your
life in the meantime,
how you make decisions when you
don't know for sure what's next.
What you do with yourself between
the last time you heard from God
and the next time you hear from God is
the ongoing challenge of the life of faith.*

—CeCe Winans,
On a Positive Note

There are five small words in Scripture quite often overlooked and severely minimized by most readers upon a casual reading of the Bible— "In the course of time." The words appear innocent enough, simply transitioning the reader into the next chapter of God's story. However, these five small words, many times, cradle years of unseen faithful endurance on the part of the character, as God strengthens and prepares them for what's to come.

It is easy to read stories in Scripture and think the journey was quick or easy for those choosing to walk with God. We read in a few chapters the highs and lows of a life such as Joseph or King David and think their choices to live for God and honor him were somehow easier than ours today, but this is not the case. Just like us, their lives with God were molded and shaped by how they chose to trust him through the daily challenges of life.

"In the course of time" or "in the meantime" is when God does some of his best work, teaching his children how to live faithfully with him and more fully trust him when they don't know what is to come or how their story will progress. It is in the ordinary "meantime" of everyday living where God reveals his character and faithfulness to those seeking to live surrendered to him. It is not always easy, but "in the meantime" is quite often where God demonstrates the sustaining power of his presence as more than enough to comfort his children in the unknowns of what lie ahead.

It had been less than five months since our marriage had exploded when Todd and I chose to give up all that was familiar and follow the unseen nudges of God to Texas. At first, it seemed like a grand adventure and hope for a new beginning, which it was. However, we were not prepared for the difficulties of the transition that lay ahead. Both of our hurts and old natures had not just magically disappeared because of sunshine, palm trees, and Jesus. Thankfully, God went with us, and once there, the real work began as we learned to love, forgive, trust again, and do ordinary life with God and each other "in the meantime" of our healing.

§

Pulling into our new apartment complex in Texas, I felt a mixture of excitement and exhaustion for what lay ahead. It had already been two very long days of driving, stopping frequently to let the kids stretch their legs, but we had made it. Todd had driven the twenty-six-foot U-Haul truck, and I drove the car, both packed tightly with the remnants of our old life. The kids loved riding in the "big truck" and had spent most of the drive with Todd as I followed behind. I found myself grateful for the alone time to process and pray about all that had transpired and to let the tears of fear, hope, hurt, sadness, and joy flow. But with each passing mile marker, I became more and more aware of how far we were from family and how alone we would be with no one but each other to lean on. I wondered, "How in the world are we going to make it?"

Upon parking, the kids jumped out of the truck, both eager to know which apartment was ours and when they could see the pool and go swimming. Squatting down to their level, Todd pointed up to the window on the third floor, smiling as he spoke, "That one right there is ours!" Immediately, the kids ran to the open stairwell at the front of the building, leading to the third floor, Sydney screaming, "Come on, come on, let's go see it!" Todd and I quickly followed, grateful for the kids' excitement in the face of such tremendous change.

The apartment was great but would be a significant lifestyle change for our family. It was only two bedrooms, which meant the kids would share a room, and two baths with a small living room, galley kitchen, and dining area that barely fit the four of us around the table. It was definitely "cozy" and would not allow any of us the space to hide from each other, which in hindsight, I believe was part of God's process for us to rebuild. Still, it would be a major adjustment as we learned to reconnect as a couple and a family in the minutiae of daily life.

Apartment life in Texas brought its joys and challenges. The complex pool was amazing, and we spent as much time there as possible with the kids or riding bikes around the grounds. The third floor, however, proved to be problematic. Hauling groceries for four people up three flights of stairs while watching two children was not easy or fun. There was no washer or dryer in our apartment either, so we had to utilize the laundry room on site. Carrying several loads of clothes up and down three flights of stairs and across the entire complex was an unexpected chore. Then there was the surprise of our building being in the midst of the gorgeous towering Texas pine trees, which housed the most ridiculously large wood roaches I'd ever seen! The first one revealed itself to me in the apartment while running across the front of the television. So gross!

Then there was adjusting to the weather. We loved the Texas heat, and still do, but had much to learn about navigating it in the summer months. Back in Missouri, I could just throw my groceries in the trunk and head home after shopping, but in the Texas heat, milk would spoil in the quarter-mile drive home without a cooler.

I was not happy about that lesson. Towels had to be left in the car at all times because the kids would burn their little legs on the leather seats and apparently, crayons would easily melt all over those leather seats as well if left out in the car by accident. Yet another fun lesson.

I realize what a baby I sound like as I recall these issues. I know in and of themselves, none of these things are terrible. Definitely first-world problems and so insignificant in the grand scheme of things plaguing our world like poverty, health crisis, global warming, child abuse, etc. I am also aware that after all Todd and I had been through leading up to this point, this stuff was trivial in comparison, but that is why this part of our story is so important. The small stuff, the day in and day out of daily life is what we had no idea of how to navigate with each other or with God. This trivial stuff is what revealed our deep roots of selfishness, impatience, frustration, bitterness, meanness, and distrust of one another. In the small stuff, God was teaching us things we would need to help us heal from the big stuff. If we could learn to be kind, compassionate, sensitive, and forgiving in the irritating everyday moments of life, maybe, just maybe we could begin to extend those graces to healing from our past.

It sounds so eloquent to say and yet so very difficult to live out with someone, that deep down, you are unsure about trusting.

కి

The day in and day out of building a new life in Texas brought a welcomed distraction from the focus on our relationship. It was refreshing, for a time, to put on hold the hard conversations about the past and to look forward to the future. We were both very aware that we would have to return to them at some point, as the daily frustrations of life continued to reveal our lingering hurt, but for a while, our focus became adjusting to our new life. It is in these adjustments, God began to reveal his presence, showing us with immense clarity that he had indeed been the one to bring us to Texas and that he would sustain us.

The first order of business was to find a permanent home and get Sydney into school before the start of the year. It was incredibly important to us not to put her in one school district and then move her to another when we found a house. The kids had experienced so much change already, and we desperately wanted to provide them with stability. Our apartment was a month-to-month lease, so we immediately found a realtor and started searching. We arrived in Texas on July 1 and school started August 10. Was it even possible to make this happen?

Daily, I would search with the realtor while Todd worked and on the weekends take him to see the top candidates. It only took a few weeks, but we found a home in an affordable area we loved in a neighboring city. It was not fancy, just a basic ranch with a big backyard, but we immediately loved it and moved forward. There was much excitement to have found a place to settle but also trepidation as we would not close until mid-August. What should we do about Syd and school? This would be our first endeavor into prayer together.

Pouring your heart and mind out to God in prayer can be a very intimate act. Still not trusting Todd with my heart, I was not prepared to let him into this area of my life. Talking to God was sacred and special to me, and at that time, I did not think Todd was worthy of sharing in that part of my life. I did not verbalize this to him, as it felt unnecessary. He was still figuring out God for himself and prayer was new to do even on his own in private. So it was basically a brief conversation led by me saying, "Hey, we should really pray about this and see if God can help." Todd agreed, and we each did our own thing in that realm.

To our utter surprise, God came through! In talking to the school district about our situation, they agreed, very unprecedentedly, to allow Sydney to start school on August 10 as long as I could provide a valid contract and proof of our closing date later that month. They even said I could drive her to the neighborhood that first week so she could begin riding the bus and get into a regular rhythm. We could not deny God's hand in orchestrating this and saw immediately how important prayer was going to be in building a new foundation for our family.

❦

The next order of business once in our new home was finding a church. We had popped into a few different ones over the past month but not looked for anything permanent until we knew where our home would be. Now that we were getting more settled this felt like a priority. Neither of us had any real idea how to find a church home, so I called Pastor Larry back in Missouri, and he gave me some guidance and suggestions of what to look for in a church.

There seemed to be a church on every corner in Texas, so it was a bit overwhelming at first. To make it easy, we decided to simply search for Bible churches and see where that would take us. We tried two or three initially that were "okay" but finally landed at one that felt like a good fit. It was a little further away than we would have liked, twenty minutes on a slow Sunday morning, but everyone was friendly, and we both connected well with the messages. It was there that God would begin to truly bring healing, amazing friends, and hope for what we could be as a couple and a family.

Once we committed to the church, we requested a meeting with the senior pastor. Pastor John was in his first year as the new senior pastor and as down to earth as you can get. He was kind, caring, and loved Jesus, but otherwise a polar opposite from Pastor Larry. While Pastor John wore a suit while preaching, the rest of the time you found him in jeans and a T-shirt, which made him feel like a regular guy Todd could relate to about life. This made it easier to open up quickly and share about everything that had happened in our story and how we had landed in Texas.

I remember our first meeting fondly. I'm not sure what Pastor John expected when we sat down on the couch in his office that day, but clearly, it was not what we shared. He sat, intently listening and nodding his head to reveal he was following us, but when we finally finished sharing, he just stared at us. Finally, he broke the silence and with much humility said, "Thank you for sharing your story with me, but what is it you want me to do for you?"

Reaching over, I grabbed Todd's hand, looked at him with kindness, then looking back at Pastor John said, "Disciple him. We don't know how to do this. I don't know how to teach him how to be a Christian husband and father."

With a nod, Pastor John smiled and said, "Okay. Todd, let's get something on the books and we'll go from there."

That day with Pastor John was so far removed from what I had experienced as a little girl sitting with my mom in her pastor's office, being shamed for her husband's indiscretions. It was full of love, grace, humility, and understanding. For me, it was a behind-the-scenes moment of healing that no one else would see or know but God knew my little girl's heart desperately needed. God was redeeming this broken part of my story and, unknown to me at the time, preparing me to love other broken people through their pain in the future.

❧

God had asked me to stay in my broken marriage to show Todd he was real, and "in the course of time," that began to happen. We had moved to Texas from Missouri, found a home, settled in a church, and began to rebuild our family around a new life with God at the center. Todd had come to faith in Jesus, and we had found a caring church home. It sounds so very simple, seamless, and easy, doesn't it? Clearly, God was moving on our behalf, but to leave you with this imagery alone is to betray the truth of the narrative. God was present and he was working, but more than anything, during this time, he was insulating us with his presence as we fought for our family in the tension of the healing process.

Upon arrival at our apartment, we had to immediately unpack our moving truck to avoid late charges if it wasn't returned later that day. With no family or friends around to help, Todd and I would have to carry everything up three flights of stairs by ourselves. There was bickering and irritation with one another. I wasn't strong enough to do the work he needed me to do, which left him cranky and physically exhausted. A small wooden kitchen console revealed how far we had to go in being kind to one another. I had moved it to the end of the truck but failed to stabilize the legs on the liftgate. Hopping off to wait for him to help me take it down, the gate wobbled and the piece of furniture fell off the truck, shattering it on the pavement. Todd's anger flared and fear immediately crept in, whispering, "See, he hasn't changed, he's still the same old angry guy as before." I wondered, what is a red flag of him being the same and what is giving him grace as he grows?"

Further tensions arose as we were learning to live on a third of our previous income. There was no extra money for eating out or splurging in any way. Before, both of us could spend within reason however we wanted. Now, every dollar had to be accounted for, and we had to check with one another if we were spending any amount over fifty dollars. Questions arose surrounding wants versus needs, the kid's picky eating habits, the price of Kellogg's Pop-Tarts vs. the Aldi toaster pastries, and which places were cheaper to get gas. It was painful and stressful but forced us to unite in our finances. We could each dig our heels in and try to force our own agenda or we could learn, with God's help, to manage our money together.

An overwhelming sense of melancholy hit me for the first time during this transition. I had never experienced anything like it before and had no frame of reference to deal with the monster that would later be labeled as depression. My family was together and trying to rebuild; I should have been happy about that, but daily I would wake with a cloud of sadness hovering over me. I could not articulate to Todd why I wanted to cry for no reason, and while he tried to offer comfort, he simply couldn't understand, which brought more tension in our relationship.

Then there was the constant fear during this time of me simply feeling stupid about believing God could fix us. It was always one step forward and two steps back. I'd see glimmers of positive change in Todd and then moments of his old nature creeping up. There was nothing awful, inappropriate, or anything to do with another woman, just overwhelming fear of us never moving forward when there were normal moments of human anger, frustration, or disappointment displayed in him. Fear would grip me in those moments with such overwhelming, out-of-proportion intensity that all I wanted to do was give up. The only thing that kept me going was remembering God asking me to stay and my saying yes. As hard as the relationship was, I did not want to disappoint God by giving up.

Intimacy was built with God in those dark moments of sharing my hurt, frustration, and fears with him. The epitome of this was the day I found myself laying on the bathroom floor, engulfed in tears because of an argument between Todd and I about him wanting to stay home to watch football on Sunday rather than attend a church event with me. In the big scheme of things, this was truly no big deal, but to my still healing heart, it felt like my world was crumbling. Laying there on the cold tile, head propped up on the wadded bathroom rug I prayed, "Lord, what am I supposed to do? I think I've totally screwed myself. I told you I would stay and try to forgive and now I just don't want to. How do I get out of this?"

No whisper came from God at that moment, but what I did experience was the warmth of his presence and safety in sharing with him so honestly. I wondered as I prayed, "Can I even say the word "screwed" to God in a prayer?" I rationalized, "Well, this is how I would share these thoughts with a close friend, and he knows everything I'm thinking anyway, so why not?"

Unknown to me at the time, a deep friendship with my Savior was beginning to take root in that moment. Like any good friend, as I lay there talking to him, his Spirit brought clarity to me. He allowed my mind to see the disparagement in my thinking about my argument with Todd and to remember how far we had truly come in the midst of tremendous adversity. Yes, there was still more healing needed but one argument was not going to destroy our progress.

Pulling myself up off the floor, I felt comforted by God, but also an internal sense of shame. Peering into the bathroom mirror, wiping the smeared mascara from my eyes, I chastised myself, "What is wrong with you? God has fought so hard for you and your family. Why are you doubting?" I thought for certain God had to be disappointed in me but soon he would show me this was not the case.

My heart warms in the afterglow of the mercy I received that day as I consider all God revealed to me during that time through the life of the prophet Elijah in 1 Kings chapters 17–19. This is someone who *knew* God, whose faith was so strong and powerful that his prayers brought and stopped a three-year drought. He even prayed so powerfully that fire fell from heaven at his asking. I don't think anyone could ask for clearer evidence that God was with them and working on their behalf, and yet later in his story, we read of him feeling so overwhelmed and fearful that he asks God to take his life. We can sugarcoat it, but his language is clearly suicidal in nature, "I have had enough, Lord," he said. "Take my life" (1 Kings 19:4 NIV). The journey had been too much and he was done. I could definitely relate.

When I first read his story, I imagined God getting so very angry at Elijah for his self-pity and doubt in the face of discouragement. How in the world could this amazing prophet give up after all the things he had witnessed God do? How could he be so fearful and done with life after all the miracles God had performed through him? Certainly, God would be justified in giving Elijah a severe reprimand, at least that's what my humanness concluded.

Interestingly enough, that is *not* how God responded to Elijah. Instead, he sent an angel to bring him food and water, telling him to get some rest. Once Elijah is past his physical exhaustion, God allows him to speak, to vent, and share the fear and distortions his mind has made him think about his situation. With compassion, God listens to his hurting child without expressing disappointment and without shaming him. Then, when the time is right, through a gentle whisper, God reveals the power of his presence and empowers Elijah to get up and get back to the work at hand. What a beautifully merciful picture of God.

As I learned more about Elijah's life, what I came to know is that the same God who loved this prophet through his mental breakdown centuries ago was the same God who loved me that day on my bathroom floor. No, I was not a prophet who could call down fire from heaven, but I was God's child and had heard his whisper on two occasions and witnessed his hand sustaining my marriage and family to that point. I had experienced more than enough of God to know the power of prayer and to see him do the miraculous. Still, God reminded me through Elijah that I was human and the journey to that point had been arduous. Just because I loved God, my humanity, susceptibility to fatigue, depression, and fear had not magically been erased.

For too long after that day, I carried shame, viewing myself as nothing more than a flaky little doubting disappointment to God, whining on the bathroom floor. But "in the course of time" through his word and Elijah's story, God enabled me to forgive myself for my human discouragement, eventually erasing the shame I felt that day.

"Life in the meantime" is where our faith began to take root as Todd and I were learning how to consistently do life with God. As we invited him into all aspects of our lives "in the meantime" of healing, God began to prepare both Todd and me for deeper levels of restoration in areas beyond the affair. During this time, we were learning to love again and forgive each other, but also ourselves in the process. God would need us to be strong for what lie ahead and forgiving ourselves would open both of us up to the honesty that would be necessary. What came next would require new levels of vulnerability with each other and the humility of inviting others into our past brokenness and current struggle to move forward. Thankfully, God already had the support we needed ready and prepared us to enter into it.

11

Building Community

We may be called into or choose
a particular community,
but once we are in community,
the brothers and sisters are given.
Some will get on our nerves, others will attract us.
But community means caring for each one.

—Jean Vanier,
From Brokenness to Community

Entering into a Christian community and building safe friendships is a task that is surprisingly more difficult than many expect. The human perspective rationalizes, churches are filled with nice people who love God, therefore, those I meet will be kind, accepting, and safe with my heart, the brokenness of my past, and my hopes for the future. Unfortunately, this is not always the case, leaving many discouraged and disillusioned by the people they encounter in the Christian community of the church.

The problem, however, is not simply with the people, rather with our expectations of them. How easily we forget that those who follow Jesus are not perfect and that they, too, have broken parts of their stories just like us. They, too, are in process with God, but because we expect more from them, we downplay signs of unsafety in these people like a critical spirit, not keeping confidence, or simply being judgmental or unkind. We overlook these shortcomings because we believe God calls us to love, but do so to the detriment of our own mental and spiritual health.

Finding safe friendships at church is ultimately about discernment and using the wisdom God has given us. Yes, he calls us to love, but he also very clearly tells us in Proverbs 4:23 (NIV, 1984), "Above all else, guard your heart, for it is the wellspring of life." It is possible to love well while guarding our hearts at the same time, but we have to be intentional about doing so. Our flesh will naturally want to pull away from difficult people at church, but they may be the ones God wants us to walk alongside for a season. This, however, doesn't mean we open up our entire life to them with no boundaries. There will also be those we do feel safe with and we may want to hide our past or current struggles out of fear, but this too may be exactly where God wants us to find help, hope, and healing.

Building a healthy Christian community can be a struggle, but it is an area where God meets us as we surrender it to him. His Holy Spirit is faithful to guide us in discernment; the challenge is paying attention to his flutters in our chest that nudge us when we are to speak up and when we are to stay silent. Heeding these nudges can be the difference between life change and stagnation.

God already had brothers and sisters in Christ ready for Todd and me to do life with at our new church, even before we arrived. Some of them would become life-long friends, teaching us what true loving Christian friendship is all about. They would support us, challenge us, pray for us, and become like family. Others would teach us how to love and do life together while paying attention to the Spirit's promptings to guard our hearts. Every person would shape who we were becoming as followers of Jesus, teaching us how to love and be loved in return.

ৎ

Prior to our Texas move, I had never had a true Christian friendship. Yes, I'd known other Christians at various times in life who you might label as a friend but never a true Christian friendship where you shared life, prayed for each other, and talked about how God was intersecting your story without fear of being seen as a Jesus freak. My heart desperately longed for this kind of friendship, so once we began to find some semblance of stability in our new life, I began to pray for a Christian friend.

Since God had already done so much for us to this point, I set the bar pretty low, praying, "Lord, if you could just give me one Christian friend, just one, I'd be so grateful." To my surprise, he would bring many in the years to come. The first one, however, he would bring right to my front door.

Mike and Kim had moved into our neighborhood the week before we arrived and three years later would move away a week before we left. This was clearly a God-ordained friendship for this specific season of our life. Kim was a stay-at-home mom with three children under the age of four, and her husband Mike was in the military. They were the first "normal" family we had met as a couple who followed Jesus and were instrumental in showing Todd and I how to live out our faith while going about the normal tasks of working, raising a family, and healing from our past.

It was solely by God's providence that we met. They, too, had decided to make our new church their church home as well, but having two large services every Sunday, we could have easily never met. Interestingly, they had signed up for the same parenting class Todd and I had already decided to take. The class required all participants to watch an introductory video before the first session, and I had the VHS tape (well before the convenience of digital media).

One day, as I went about my daily tasks at home, the doorbell rang, and to my surprise, a strange woman stood at my doorstep. "Hey there!" Kim said in a thick southern drawl as I opened the door, "My husband and I are taking the parenting class at church and they said you had the intro video. Since we live just a few streets over, I thought I'd stop by and see if you were done with it?"

The class administrator had already called and asked me if she could give my address to someone who needed the video; I just had not expected her to show up so soon. The introvert in me does not do well with strangers, even those I know who may be coming, but Kim was warm and friendly, making it easy to connect. This first interaction was brief, the equivalent of pleasantries and the exchange of the video through the door, but it would be the beginning of a friendship that would teach me how to be a friend and what to look for in a Christian friendship for the rest of my life.

∽

God's choice of Kim to be my first Christian friend was a beautiful reflection of his tender love and care for my healing heart during that time. While Kim was a normal woman who loved Jesus, she also held a master's degree in psychology, with some PhD work under her belt, which meant she simply knew how to sit with me and listen well when I finally shared with her our story of broken-ness. There was no feeling of judgment or condemnation in our interactions and no trying to "fix" on her part, just the safety of a friend listening and coming to know more of our story.

Early on, I struggled internally with the dynamics of our friendship because I felt as though I was taking far more than I was giving. Her family seemed so stable, and mine was such a wreck. Life was slowly improving for Todd and me, but the cloud of mel-ancholy that followed me was palpable. I was keenly aware that she was receiving a very inadequate version of me as a friend, and I hated that for her. I wanted to love and support her the way she gave that to me, but so often felt I was falling short as a friend. Not once did she ever complain. In fact, what she did more often than not was lean in further to help me find hope.

Kim's winning quality was knowing how to "speak the truth in love." She had the ability, unlike anyone I'd ever met, to tell you exactly what she was thinking, even if it was hard to hear, with love and care. This made it easier to share with her because you never had to wonder what she was thinking; she would soon tell you. But even though I'd come to trust her, I found myself holding back in the area of my sadness. I was so afraid to share with her the depths of my despair for fear she would think that I wasn't trusting God. When I finally found the courage to open up to her about it, I was once again met with eyes of kindness and words of encouragement as she said, "Steph, this has been such a difficult journey for you. The fact that you are still standing is a miracle! You did what you needed to do to survive and save your family. Now that life is getting better, your body needs to release the emotion and sadness of it all."

My heart felt a sense of relief in her words, and I responded, "Okay, so what am I supposed to do? Some days I can hardly function."

With a big smile and a small chuckle carrying her words she said, "Oh, honey, you can love Jesus and still take an antidepressant. You need to go see your doctor." And so I did.

Kim was the first person to ever talk with me about matters of faith and mental health. She helped me to see that loving Jesus did not magically take away the biological effects that stress had placed on my body over the past year and that it was okay to seek help. I was grateful for her wisdom, and though I hated the label of depression that would follow my doctor's visit, I was glad to know I was not somehow failing God or lacking in faith. In fact, what I came to see was God's wisdom and guidance in the medical industry providing insight on medications and tools for healing. So I took the antidepressant, began to feel better, and a year later weaned off them once in a place of consistent stability. Had I needed to remain on them, I would have, knowing sometimes this is a biological necessity. Our brain is an organ like our heart, lungs, kidneys, etc., and unfortunately, there are times when it just doesn't function the way it's supposed to, but that was not part of my journey.

ॐ

Mark and Belinda would be the next couple to enter our story, teaching us much about hospitality, generosity, and following the Spirit's nudges. We had randomly sat next to them at a church dinner in the fall, for no other reason than there were four seats available at their table. They were older than us by about twenty-five years, but very nice and engaging to chat with about being new to Texas. The evening was pleasant, and for the first time, it felt like we were just a normal family meeting new people at church. We talked about so many things over dinner and, by the end of the

119

evening, felt like friends. Upon hearing that we had no family in the area, they invited us to join them for Thanksgiving dinner at their home and thus began our friendship.

Hospitality and generosity were both definitive spiritual gifts of Mark and Belinda. They clearly did very well for themselves financially as was evidenced by their large home, pool, and cars but never came across as snooty or elite. Instead, what they modeled was a life that shared their abundance with others—our family quite often being on the receiving end. On many occasions, we were invited to holiday gatherings, dinners, or even just the use of their pool with the kids. When you were their guest on any occasion, you never received the bare minimum, always more than you would expect. Whether it was food, drink, or time, they were always ready to share more.

The dynamics of our friendship with Mark and Belinda were quite interesting. While Todd and I felt loved and cared for by them, we both felt a hesitation about sharing certain parts of our story with them. We had been extremely open with them about having marital problems and struggling as a family but never spoke directly about Todd's affair or my past indiscretions. There were a few occasions when we came close, but each time something got in the way. "Something just doesn't feel right," was a phrase we both used to describe why we held back, but we couldn't pinpoint exactly why we felt that way. The block in our sharing with them was consistent enough that Todd and I took notice. We were still very new to deep matters of faith but felt like the Holy Spirit was definitely saying "no" to opening up with them about this part of our story, so we eventually stopped trying.

Years later, we saw God's protection of our hearts through this simple act of obedience in following the Holy Spirit's lead, not to share all the details of our story.

Sitting with Mark and Belinda over dinner, only a few weeks before we were scheduled to move, the conversation turned to a couple in our church who had recently experienced the sting of infidelity. They were trying to heal, but the details of the indiscretion were very public and the situation ugly. Not wanting to gossip,

I tried to change the subject with a simple offer of positivity. "Well, there's always hope. God can heal anything," I said with a small smile, glancing over at Todd.

In a condescending tone, interpreted by me as meaning I was too young to understand these kinds of things, Mark said very dogmatically, "No. These kinds of situations never heal."

I wanted to honor our friends and the invitation into their home but felt compelled to push back a bit. "That seems a little skeptical, don't you think?" I said with as much kindness as I could muster.

"No, it's not skeptical, it's just reality," said Belinda, very matter of fact, continuing, "Mark and I were both cheated on in our first marriages, and neither was salvageable. So no, we don't have much hope for situations of infidelity. Once a cheater, always a cheater."

Todd sat quietly before responding, "I'm sorry that was part of your story."

"It's okay," Belinda said as she stood up to clear the table. Placing her hand on Mark's shoulder, she continued, "We've been married for a long time now and have a good marriage."

Driving away from their home that night, Todd and I were both very aware of how God had guarded our healing hearts early on in this friendship. "I guess we were right not to share that part of our story. I'm not sure how they would have responded," I said with sadness in my voice.

"Yeah, I don't know," Todd said in agreement. Clearly, both Mark and Belinda had been wounded by their previous spouse's choices. Maybe they would have loved us well if we'd shared, but maybe not. All we knew is that God had directed us not to share and heeding his warnings allowed us to do life with good friends while protecting our hearts in the process.

༄

Ida, Ann, and Dena were the unique trio of women God brought to love and encourage my young heart as I grew in matters of faith. All three were followers of Jesus and each in very differ-

121

ent stages of life than me. Ida and Dena were both in their forties, married, with older children. Though their husbands were open to matters of faith, they did not regularly attend church with them. Ann was in her sixties, widowed, with adult children. It was an odd group of women to connect with, being that I wasn't yet thirty, and yet they were precisely who God knew I needed during this time.

I first met them at a weekly women's Bible study, hosted in the home of one of the women's ministry leaders from the church. This was my first attempt at doing anything like this, and I was intimidated, but knowing I wanted to build friendships I decided to give it a try. The group was roughly eight to twelve women in various stages of life from their twenties to their seventies, and the evenings were not overly structured or theologically heavy. We simply arrived, grabbed coffee or tea, discussed the previous week's home study topic, and then broke for appetizers and socialization before leaving, typically after two hours.

I found great solace in these evenings. As my relationship issues with Todd were continuing to heal, I was once again diving deep into my relationship with God and loved having people to learn from about matters of faith. At first, I very rarely shared but, over time, felt more comfortable opening up about what I was learning in private and in our time together, though I never shared about our personal struggles. As the study drew to a close, Ida, Ann, and Dena asked if I'd be interested in meeting weekly to do a book or Bible study with them. Without hesitation, I said yes.

The first six months of our time together were amazing. Whatever we chose to study, I dove into 100 percent, bringing all kinds of insights and questions to every discussion. I'd never had friends I could sit and ponder hard questions with about God and faith and it was so good for my soul. Each and every week, my heart was once again falling deeper in love with God and his word and in my enthusiasm, I would bring that excitement to our meetings. At first, my hope was well received, but I remember the day that shifted.

We had met at a local Indian restaurant for dinner and our discussion. The air was thick with the delicious smell of curry, and I was once again excited to share about what God had been teaching me that week. We had already ordered and were exchanging pleasantries as we waited for our food when the evening took a turn. I had made a comment about being so excited to share what I'd been learning when I saw Ida, Ann, and Dena slyly glance at one another, giving subtle nods, indicating something was coming.

Slowly reaching her hand across the table to grasp mine, Ann smiled as she tenderly spoke, "Stephanie, we love you, and we are so excited about all the God is doing in your life and your family, and all that he is teaching you. We really are excited for you." Pause. "We're just not sure this is the right group for you anymore. You see, you have no idea what it's like to have such a broken past or to struggle in your marriage and family the way we have at times. Your life just seems so together and ours is not."

Tears filled my eyes and my heart began to pound wildly in my chest as I internally screamed, "What? No idea? Are you kidding me? No, you guys have no idea of all that I've been through, how broken my past, my marriage, and my family have been, or why I'm now clinging to God so fiercely these days!" I could feel my face now beginning to flush as I tried to swallow the lump forming in my throat. Searching for words to respond, the pounding increased in my chest as I once again heard the familiar whisper in my soul, "Steph, tell them."

All this time, I had kept the brokenness of my story tightly tucked away in my heart, sharing only with a select few, believing that somehow, I was honoring God by only showing those in the church this happy, shiny, perfect, growing Christian wife and mother. At this moment with these women, God gently revealed to me how wrong my thinking had been and then taught me the lesson that would forever change the way I would enter into Christian community as he once again whispered, "Steph, tell them. It is *impossible* for you to share the fullness of your joy without sharing the fullness of your sorrow. Tell them your story." And so I did.

Sitting there for hours, I shared about all Todd and I had been through and all the ways God had been speaking over the years, drawing me closer to trust, healing, and hope in the most hopeless of situations. By the end of our conversation, a deeper bond was formed as they now knew what fed my tenacity for God and a new appreciation for each of our stories and struggles had been forged. Weekly, we would continue to meet for the next few years until I moved, growing in friendship, faith, and love for one another.

෨

Of all the people God brought into my life during this season, Marianne was by far the most surprising. We met at the same women's Bible study where I'd previously met Ida, Ann, and Dena, and I loved to hear her talk about Jesus. Marianne was in her seventies, and most definitely not your typical old crotchety follower of Jesus. No, she was different—so spry and fiery in her faith, inviting you to want what she had simply by the way she lived. I was certain she must have been one of those people who'd known God her whole life by the way she talked about him.

We came to know each other on a deeper level one summer while normal church studies took a break. She offered a book study in her home, and once a month, she'd invite me to stay after for lunch. When I look back, I see how she was mentoring my young heart without intimidating me by calling it out. We'd talk about God, husbands, kids, work, ministry, and everything in between. I'd already learned my lesson from Ida, Ann, and Dena, so it was easy to invite Marianne into all aspects of my life, which she was so gracious to hold carefully.

Her wisdom in those early days of rebuilding my marriage was priceless. While I was glad for Todd's growing faith, he still had much to learn, and I would get so frustrated when I'd see parts of "old Todd" spring up. I found that when I tried to encourage him on matters of faith, it usually blew up in my face, causing an argument. Marianne had such great insight and would remind me, "Stephy, just remember, *you* are not your husband's Holy Spirit. Let God guide him and you stay out of the way." Oh, how often this insight has saved me from causing harm with Todd, my kids, and friends over the years.

Marianne was also an incredible prayer warrior, teaching me to bring *everything* to God. She encouraged me that nothing was too trivial to pray about and that it was okay to ask for help in any and every situation. For the most part, I could easily embrace this knowledge, as I'd already seen the effects prayer had on our life, but still, in healing mode, my anxiety would rise up often when Todd and I would argue. This paralyzing fear would creep in that he might change his mind about his faith and the kids and I would somehow be hurt. As I shared these fears with Marianne, she brought hope and humor, as she declared in her thick southern drawl, "Stephy, the best place you can be in your marriage is on your knees in prayer for Todd. That way when God's long arm swings by to slap him, he'll miss you!" She chuckled wildly as she said the words and then regaining her composure, gently said, "Seriously, Steph, if you are seeking God and honoring him with your life, he will protect you and your children from your husband's poor decisions."

I so loved my time with Marianne. She had such amazing knowledge and I wondered if I would ever know God the way she did or be able to connect with Scripture on her level. Clearly, this is what a lifetime spent seeking Jesus would yield. To my surprise, I was wrong about many of my assumptions. In time, Marianne would reveal to me that she hadn't come to faith in Jesus until her midfifties after the death of her husband to cancer. There was something about that part of her journey that revealed to her with much clarity how out of control life can be and how there was no one to look to for help other than God.

When she accepted Jesus, she never looked back and now dedicated her time to helping others grow in their knowledge of him as well. I was enamored with how much she knew about God in only twenty years of following him. This, strangely enough, gave me confidence that as I daily spent time with God, I too would grow in wisdom and knowledge. It was exciting to think about where I might be in my faith journey starting almost twenty-five years earlier than she and I wondered, "What might God have for me to do for him?"

∾

Ministry or counseling others was definitely not on my radar during this time, but God would use Marianne as a catalyst to begin opening my heart to the possibilities in crafty ways. I loved her summer book studies, but on more than one occasion, she would unexpectedly tell me, "Hey, Stephy, I'm gonna be out of town next week, so I've let the group know you are gonna lead the discussion." Fear would immediately paralyze me as I would defend my inadequacy and lack of knowledge, but she would just smile and say, "Let me know how it goes!"

She also recommended I lead my first Bible study at church in the fall, which was crazy intimidating. I objected profusely, "Who was I to lead a study after how jacked up my life had been?" Again, she would just smile and refuse to engage my fears, reminding me that she was there if I needed her for support. To my surprise, I loved pouring into the women and found that my past brokenness brought a tenderness to my interaction with the hard parts of Scripture that made others open to learning with me.

The biggest challenge Marianne threw me into was on my first mission trip. I'd never done anything like that before and was terrified, but she was leading and invited me to join. It was a week-long trip to provide medical and dental services to those from the most impoverished areas of Tegucigalpa, Honduras. We would set up shop in a local church and have four stations: children, medical, dental, and evangelism. The children's area was washing hair, providing lice treatments, and playing games. The medical was providing basic checkups, vitamins, or antiparasitic medications for the people whose "bellies itched from the inside" due to parasites in the local water system. Dental was cleaning or extraction, and then before leaving, everyone passed through the evangelization area to hear about the love of Jesus before leaving.

Everyone on the team was required to serve in every area. The children's area was easy and fun as I got to love on the sweetest kids. The medical and dental were more challenging as it was hard to see and hear about the physical ailments, especially of children, but my job was simply documentation and making people feel comfortable. Overall, I thought I was doing well until the night Marianne said I would need to engage the evangelism station the next day. I loved Jesus and truly believed the people of Honduras needed him, but I was *not* going to do that.

"Yeah, no, that's not really an area I'm comfortable serving in tomorrow. So I'm not gonna do that," I said directly.

Sternly, but kindly she replied, "Oh yeah, you are Steph. Everyone serves everywhere and tomorrow is your turn."

I didn't sleep at all that night. How in the world was I supposed to talk with others about Jesus with my limited knowledge and through an interpreter? The next morning came and I found myself scared, tired, and nauseous but with no choice but to go. When we arrived at the church, I was escorted to my area, which consisted of four clusters of three chairs. One for the worker, one for the interpreter, and one for the person leaving the clinic. I quickly prayed a desperate prayer for help and sat down, introducing myself to my interpreter only moments before the first person sat down. I felt so inadequate, but somehow, God brought the words I needed to offer kindness and hope. I did not push Jesus on anyone that day but reminded them of his love and the open door he provided, should they want to know him.

It was an incredibly emotionally draining day. I found that I could only sit with four or five people before I would have to excuse myself. I would then exit the building, go to a private place around back, and cry, praying desperately for wisdom that I knew I did not possess. The hurts and the needs of the people were so great, and I had no idea how to carry them or offer hope. Marianne had thrown me into the deep end of the spiritual pool, and I felt like I was drowning. But once again, to my surprise, God would provide all that I needed to endure, and I learned that day about the power of a loving presence over knowledge and skill to fix others.

৯

Every single person God brought into my life during this season was strategically placed and served a particular part in my healing journey as well as shaping my future ministry. Kim taught me the power of "speaking the truth in love" and how faith and emotional health intersect to build a healthy life. Mark and Belinda showed me the power of hospitality, generosity of spirit, and of paying attention to the Holy Spirit's guidance in relationships. Ida, Ann, and Dena taught me the necessity of authenticity and vulnerability. Marianne taught me how to love my family for Jesus while also teaching me how to stretch others on their faith journey. There are numerous others I've failed to mention but whose presence forever changed me.

Building a community of faith was not easy, but it was worth it, and to be forthcoming, future endeavors at other churches would not always yield the same depth of friendships or ease of relationships this experience brought. For us, this was very clearly a special season of love and care to strengthen us for what was to come. But what we learned was that God does some of his best work through the power of relationships, and that it is always worth the risk to do life authentically with others.

Now that we had our support in place, learning how to be open, vulnerable, and ask for help, God's voice would once again come with a request that these deep friendships would help us navigate, but first, he had one more specific request of me.

12

Forgiveness

We all know what it is like to ferociously
want something at one level
and fearfully not want it at another level.
And the odd thing is that sometimes
the more we want something, the more
we abhor the thought of having it.
It is often this way with forgiving.

—Lewis B. Smedes,
The Art of Forgiving

Forgiving someone who has deeply wounded us is one of the most Christ-like endeavors we are invited into as human beings and by far, the most impossible to do in our own strength. More than anything else, we may do in this life for God, forgiving is the one act that most clearly reflects the image of Christ in us. To forgive, as the Apostle Paul reminds us in Ephesians, is to love others as God loves us. "Be kind and compassionate to one another, forgiving each other, just as in Christ God forgave you" (Eph. 4:32 NIV). The words seem so matter-of-fact and nonchalant, just extend to others what God has already extended to you. Forgive and move on because you love Jesus. Oh, how I wish it were that simple.

There are many factors that get in the way of forgiveness, but the one that seems to plague us most when we are unwilling to forgive is a false belief that forgiveness is saying that what happened is okay. It can feel like we are simply letting someone off the hook for the harm they inflicted, which inflames our sense of justice. This, however, is not what forgiveness means. It is only through acknowledging just how much we have been wronged and the impact of that wrong that we come to the place of recognizing God's desire to release us from our wounds through forgiveness. Then, and only then, can we entrust the one who harmed us to God, allowing him to enact justice on his terms. Forgiveness brings us to a place of freedom, but not by accident.

Forgiving Todd came much more quickly than expected, but for the person with whom he'd had the affair, not so much. While I was still working toward trusting Todd again, I found that it was easier to forgive him because I could hear his words asking for forgiveness, see his remorse, and witness daily his attempts to mend what had been broken. There was absolutely none of this from the person who'd played her part in my betrayal, and I struggled with how to forgive someone who didn't seem to care how they had hurt me.

In his grace, once I was more stable, God would come seeking to mend this area of my heart. He would not make me forgive, but he would clearly invite me to it, teaching me how to allow his strength to carry me toward this impossible task.

Six to nine months into the move, a sense of stability had finally come. Our family was settled in our home, Todd's job was going well, we were building community and friendships in our new church, and daily we were growing healthier as a family. It had not been a fast or easy journey, and there was still much work to be done, but we were moving forward. For the most part, everything seemed good. I'd shared with Todd my willingness to forgive what had happened, though complete trust was still a long way off, and we both felt confident in our future. There was only one problem...Ashley.

Ashley was the name of the woman with whom Todd had the affair, and the name would immediately send me spiraling inside every time I heard it. It was like a time machine that could instantaneously transport me back in time to the moment of my deepest pain through the utterance of a simple name. I hated that name with all my heart and would go to great lengths to protect myself from hearing it if possible.

Unwilling to let me live in this space of unhealth, God would come asking me to surrender this pain too, reminding me that Jesus's name is the only one that should have any power in my life.

৵

One of the ways I attempted to build community when we first moved to Texas was to join a group of runners that were preparing for the Houston marathon. I'd read about them in the local newspaper, and apparently, it didn't matter if you were in shape or not, they would get you ready, pairing you with those who were at your same running pace. So I signed up and for five months, I would get up every Saturday morning at 5:00 a.m. to run with this group. Houston heat and humidity are no joke when running, so early was the only time to get in a run and still be able to breathe.

I had done a little running previously, but I was definitely not on the level of most of the group. A glorified jogger would most clearly describe my effort. I was an eleven-minute miler at best and there were very few in the group at my slower pace. I only needed one person to partner with, though, and she turned out to be great. The only problem was her name. Yep, it was Ashley.

When she first introduced herself to me, I was livid and remember arguing with God in my head, "Are you kidding me? I'm out here trying to get better and to make friends. How hard would it have been for you to give me a running partner with any other name? Aren't there like billions of names?" Though my anger flared at God, it was good to feel safe enough to express my frustrations to him and I wondered, "Was this intentional on his part?"

I decided to give little thought to "why" God would partner me with someone whose name brought such feelings of intense disgust and decided to do the adult thing and simply ignore it. It was ridiculous. For the entirety of five months, I never once called her by name. When we'd meet up, I'd always greet her with pleas-antries but never say her name. Whenever there was an occasion to talk about her or introduce her to someone, I'd simply say, "This is my running partner." I honestly don't know if she ever noticed, and in hindsight, it seems quite impressive to spend that much time with someone without ever saying their name. However, what it revealed more than anything was how much more healing was nec-essary and how unwilling I was to deal with it.

୭

My running partner experience didn't seem to get my atten-tion, so in time, God turned up the heat, allowing there to be someone in almost every social situation I'd enter whose name was Ashley. The name was everywhere: the gym attendant, the pediatri-cian's nurse, the Walmart checker, the Starbucks barista, etc. It was comically painful. Everywhere I went, I was confronted with this name and yet never did I consider my need to loose its power over me.

Finally, in an act of merciful intrusion, God would allow the name to enter my home, forcing me to acknowledge my need to work through this area of wounding. I recall the moment so clearly. I was cooking dinner, and Sydney came bounding into the kitchen, nibbling on the food I was preparing, jabbering on about many things, specifically the idea of being a mom herself one day, which got my attention. With much intrigue, I asked, "Really? You want to be a mommy someday?"

She smiled wide and replied emphatically, "Yep, and if I have a girl, I want to name her Ashley!"

My heart sank, but my love for my child trumped my feel-ings, so I swallowed hard and forced the words of encouragement, "That's a lovely name, sweetie. I'm sure you'll be a great mommy someday." And off she scurried having no idea how her words pierced my heart.

This seemingly insignificant interaction got my attention unlike any of those before and forced me to acknowledge to myself and God just how wounded my heart still was in certain areas. Still, what was I supposed to do? This would become the topic of many conversations with God from that day forward about how to let go and be released from the power of this name.

§

Months passed by with no resolution for my heart in this area of wounding. Despite my constant dialogue with God about it, the name Ashley continued to plague me, and I was frustrated and tired of dealing with it. Daily I wrestled inside, wondering, "Why can't I get past this?" The truth is, what I really wanted was for God to just "poof" magically make the problem disappear. I had been willing to forgive Todd, so I rationalized God should just fix this. Quid pro quo so to speak. In his mercy, however, God would not allow me to sidestep this opportunity to heal, grow, and someday help others do the same, finally intervening with a simple phone call.

Todd was at work, Syd was at school, and Cody was playing quietly in his room the morning the phone call came. I had just finished tidying up the kitchen after breakfast and the flurry of chaos that came with getting everyone ready for the day when I heard the familiar *bbbrrrriiiing* from my cell phone. Quickly, I hurried to grab it, wondering who would be calling so early. To my surprise, it was Pastor Larry's name on the screen. "Hmmm, I wonder what he wants?" I mused as I answered.

"Hey, Pastor Larry, good morning!" I said with as much enthusiasm as possible to show I was doing much better than the last time we'd spoken.

"Hey Stephanie, I'm well," he said kindly and then continued, "I was just thinking about you this morning and wanted to check in. It's been a while, so I thought I'd touch base and see how you and Todd were doing?" It was nice to hear his familiar voice, and it was effortless to share all that had transpired in the last six to nine months with the move, our new church, and the community God had placed around us. I even shared how I'd chosen to forgive Todd, and though we still had much rebuilding to do in the area of trust, we were doing well. He seemed genuinely encouraged by our progress, gave me some words of encouragement, and I thought that would bring an end to our call.

"Well, thanks so much for checking in on us," I said in the universal tone that indicates a call is over, and then God's intervention came.

"Hey, before we hang up," Pastor Larry began, "I just have one more thing. I know you are no longer part of our church, and I am technically no longer your pastor, but I've been thinking back to our many conversations and how hurt you were and I was just wondering, how are you doing with forgiveness? I mean, I know you've chosen to forgive Todd and that's great, but how are you doing with forgiving Ashley?"

I wish I could say that I received his question with openness, but I found it incredibly intrusive, thinking, *Are you kidding me? Seriously, this name* again *and now in regard to forgiveness?*

Incomprehensible! In all the months leading up to this moment, the idea of actually forgiving Ashley had never once entered my mind. Pausing for a few moments, attempting to gather my thoughts and to respond in a way that would end the conversation, I finally responded, "Good. I'm actually doing really good on that front. I mean, I understand that Jesus calls me as a follower to forgive, so I think I have and yeah, things are good."

There was another pause, this one much longer than before, and then Pastor Larry finally broke the silence, "Really?"

With all the fake confidence I could muster, I quickly retorted, "Yep, all good here."

He continued softly, "Then let me ask you this, Steph, can you wish her well? Do you want to know that she's come to know Jesus and that you'll see her in glory someday? That she's found a great husband who loves and treats her well and has a beautiful family? Can you pray blessings over her?"

With every question he posed, my heart rate began to increase and the pounding in my chest became harder and faster. I could feel my face beginning to flush and my head began to throb. On and on he seemed to go with his ridiculous questions until I couldn't take it any longer and I interrupted him in a rage, "ABSOLUTELY NOT! No! No! No! No! As far as I'm concerned, she can go straight to hell!" I was so mad that I wasn't even a bit embarrassed that I'd yelled at a pastor.

Silence once again loomed as I waited for the chastisement that was sure to come. Grasping my hands to stop them from shaking I tried to mentally prepare, but to my surprise what I heard on the other end of the line was a small chuckle. I could hear the smile in his voice as he said, "Yeah, Steph, you're not there yet! But the good news is, I know deep down you want to be, so now God has room to work. Forgiving this kind of wound takes time."

Relief filled my soul at the idea of simply "wanting to forgive" being a starting place toward forgiveness settling into my heart. That felt safe, like something I could talk to God about, and so in the weeks to come, that was how I began to pray. "Lord, help me to want to forgive Ashley." It had never occurred to me until that day it was unforgiveness giving her name power over me, and so with every prayer, I got more comfortable saying it. Eventually, it just became a name.

❧

The conversation with Pastor Larry was the catalyst that pointed me in the direction of forgiveness, but the actual act of forgiving itself took a long time and went through many phases. At first, I prayed to want to forgive, which lasted much longer than I would have thought. What helped me to move forward from this beginning stage was remembering my own past brokenness and the harm I'd caused others. This openness with myself about my own sin allowed me to begin to see Ashley as another broken human being, and I found myself wondering, "What kind of person believes that they don't deserve better than someone else's spouse?" I tried not to be harsh in my thoughts toward her, but think back to my own poor choices and remember the pain that guided them.

Seeing Ashley as another broken human being in need of God's grace allowed me to entertain the idea of forgiveness, but I would remain stuck in this place for a long time, never quite getting to the place of being able to say the words, "I forgive Ashley." I desperately wanted to say them, but just couldn't until the day Jesus gave me a "stake in the ground moment," a moment I could return to and remind myself that I had forgiven on the days my brain and feelings said otherwise.

After months of hard prayers and wrestling with God, he gave me the most beautiful moment of clarity through a dream. Now, I know that everyone dreams, but I personally rarely ever remember them, maybe only three or four to that point in my life. So when I had this dream and remembered it, I took note. It was a very ethereal image that filled my mind. Jesus was standing there in front of me, looking stereotypically himself, in a white flowing robe with a blue sash across his chest. His presence was enveloped in light, and he was looking at me with a smile. He extended his left arm out in front of himself, palm up, and there levitating above his hand was the world, slowly spinning. Looking at it, he then shifted his gaze to me and raising the globe in my direction he spoke, "Here, Steph, everything you want to do for me, it's yours. I just need you to do one thing."

Immediately I sank to my knees as I spoke, "Anything, Lord, I'll do anything you ask of me."

His words came with tenderness but also an emotion that let me know he understood how hard his request would be to hear, "I need you to forgive Ashley."

Looking at him, the world, and knowing all the desires that had been placed in my heart over the past year, the request didn't seem so hard and I thought, "Am I really going to give up everything Jesus is calling me to do for him because I want to keep this unforgiveness?"

And so, without hesitation, I replied, "Okay, Lord, I forgive Ashley."

Upon waking, I had the strangest feeling as I remembered the dream and wondered, "Was that real? Did I really forgive Ashley? I kind of think I did." I didn't share this with Todd or anyone for at least three weeks, fearing it wasn't real, but over the next few weeks, I found that I could say her name easier and considered what it may be like to pray for her. Of course, I wasn't quite there yet, but the act of forgiving had been real and I was still in process. Now, of course, I still had memories and pain associated with them. Additionally, God never imposed on me and still hasn't to this day the necessity of verbally forgiving her to her face. Forgiveness does not always mean restoration of a relationship. I have simply learned to entrust her to God and genuinely hope she's come to know him.

৯৹

If coming to forgive Ashley comes across as easy in any way, then I have failed miserably in sharing this part of my story. It was one of the hardest things the Lord has ever asked me to do and was only possible because of me surrendering to his strength within me. In and of myself, I am not capable of this kind of forgiveness. And in all truthfulness, outside of Jesus's request to do so, I probably would never have willingly wanted to forgive Ashley. Yes, that would have meant carrying around bitterness, but how quickly bitterness toward her had become a familiar friend.

The lessons that God taught me through this request to forgive Ashley were twofold. First, Jesus could be trusted. If he was asking me to do something, it was not simply because it was a rule or a command that he required me to obey. It was because he loved me and knew the freedom that would come into my life once I released this bitterness and unforgiveness to him. His request was offering mercy not only to Ashley but more so to my heart.

The second thing this request taught me was an extension of what I'd already been learning thus far with Jesus, which was, it was only love for him that could equip me to follow him with such obedience. No motivation, other than love for Jesus, could ever provide the necessary strength to offer this kind of forgiveness and mean it. Fear of not being seen as a good Christian, being a rule follower, or even not doing what the Bible said, was not motivation enough to follow through with forgiveness. The only thing that allowed me to say yes was my love for Jesus and ultimately not wanting to disappoint him, as my friend.

Relationship, not religion, is what Jesus wanted from me and is what he was teaching me in each area of life he asked me to surrender. Now that these lessons were learned and good friends were in place, his final request came not just to me but to Todd as well.

13

Nothing Left Hidden

*Jesus goes out of his way to prepare
my heart to listen and learn.
He waits for the moment I'm most ready to obey.
And while I can still refuse him at
any time, his rebuke is gentle.
It woos me at the same time it disarms me,
making me willing and open and ready to change.*

—Joanna Weaver,
Having a Mary Heart in a Martha World

Dreaming with God is a holy endeavor that I've found very few Christians allow themselves to pursue. The reasons why are plentiful, but the most common objection I hear is, "Who am I to do anything for God?" While I understand the resistance, my answer is simple and direct, "You are no one and he wants you anyway; broken as you are, he can use you for his glory if you let him." While this is true, there is, however, another prevalent reason accompanying the resistance of dreaming with God—the cost.

Opening our hearts and minds to the purposes God may have for our lives is a terrifyingly vulnerable place to be. Our human mind floods us with so many questions. "What if God asks me to move to Africa and become a missionary? What if he asks me to give more money to the church? What if he asks me to do something I simply do not want to do?" The "what ifs" are so overwhelming that it becomes safer to simply not dream with God, and so we settle for a good, but stunted version of the life that could be if we chose to trust his plans and purposes.

Nearly a year had passed since God allowed the crushing blows that shattered my life, my marriage, and my family. In that time, he had done miraculous healing in my heart and mind, giving me the strength to trust him and the grace to walk with him through what seemed like impossible requests. Though I struggled greatly along the way, he remained faithful, meeting me at every step, providing tools, help, hope, and encouragement, finally, bringing me to a place of peace. Life was not perfect, but I could finally breathe again, which allowed me to begin to dream for the first time ever about what my life could be for him.

It was becoming clear to me, and those around me, that in the midst of everything that had transpired, God was calling me into the world of ministry. While I was not willing to let my past brokenness deter me, there was an awareness of something that needed to be done before I could move forward and I was terrified. I could sense the Holy Spirit daily nudging me to deal with a few things left hidden from my past but I was unsure if after all we had been through it was worth it to go digging around there again. Still, the Spirit kept coming, gently nudging, wanting to unearth anything that lay hidden with the power to do harm in the future. It was not an easy decision, and I wondered, "Would the cost outweigh the benefits?" Though I had witnessed God do so much with my obedience already, I still wasn't convinced.

Life, for the first time in many, many years, was good. My marriage had finally moved past the point of simply surviving and was beginning to actually grow. The kids were settled, happy, and thriving in our new Texas life. And I was finding a growing sense of purpose in the world of women's ministry at our church. Joy, which had been an elusive concept to me in the past, had finally found me, and I was hopeful for what my future might be. Of course, this is when the Holy Spirit came calling with yet another area to surrender—the past...all of it.

During this season, God had begun to provide more opportunities for me to teach Bible studies, and I found that, though I was scared and intimidated much of the time, I loved pouring into the lives of women. I had no idea what God might have for me, but my heart was open and I longed to see the possibilities. To my surprise, as I began to allow myself to dream with God about what a future in ministry might look like, thoughts of my past began to haunt me. At first, it was ugly accusations from within, "Who are you to do anything for God after the mess you've made of your life? You don't know enough about God to help others. Who would even listen to you?" These questions were fair, but inadequate obstacles as God had already shown me the power of his mercy and forgiveness, so I pushed forward.

Still, the past continued to come calling. As I'd sit across the table from a woman at coffee, trying to lovingly encourage her to trust God with everything, the thought would come, "Well, Todd doesn't know everything about your past, and you aren't trusting God with that information." I'd quickly try to push it out of my head, chalking it up to the enemy trying to destroy what God was doing in my life, justifying, "Todd doesn't need to know every detail about my past." Or I'd be teaching a study about not letting fear have power in our lives when the whisper would come, "Umm, you are terrified of certain things from your past leaking out, how can you tell these women this?" These thoughts were pervasive, coming with every opportunity I had to minister to others and I didn't know what to do.

The truth is, not every hidden thing in our past needs to be revealed. Sometimes, it is enough to know God has forgiven us and to move forward without causing further harm to others. The question for me during this time was whether God was asking me to reveal these things or whether the enemy was simply trying to wreak havoc and do harm? All I knew was I had to figure out the answer and quickly because daily my stomach was in knots.

৯

After weeks of wrestling with my fears by myself, finally, I decided to reach out to Marianne. Over lunch, I shared everything that was weighing on my heart and mind and waited for God's wisdom to speak through her as it had so many times before. Sitting across the table, the remains of lunch now long gone, she remained silent for a time before finally speaking. "Stephy," she began compassionately, "Romans 8:1 says, 'There is now no condemnation for those who are in Christ Jesus.'" Looking deep into her gaze, I nodded in agreement. She continued, "So how does the voice that is whispering to you sound?"

"What do you mean?" I asked, feeling a bit confused.

Smiling, she elaborated, "Well, the voice of God is never going to make you feel stupid or ashamed, for there is now no condemnation for those who are in Christ Jesus. Oh, he'll definitely nudge you if you are doing something wrong, but never to shame you or talk down to you. So is the voice you hear in those moments of doing ministry kind or accusing?"

As I sat thinking about it, I realized that it was a bit of both. "Well," I said, "the voice that says, 'Who are you to do anything for God after the mess you've made of your life?' is accusatory, that's why I shut it down so quickly."

"Yes, that's good," she said, nodding with approval. "God would never speak to you like that."

"But the other whispers I hear inside my head aren't harsh, they just feel true. Like, how can I tell others to trust God completely when I'm still living in fear?" I said with a note of sadness.

"Stephy, honey, I think that's the Holy Spirit," Marianne spoke gently. "Maybe he wants you to have nothing left hidden in your marriage?"

I couldn't explain it, but knew she was right as I interjected, "But why? Why now? What is the purpose of sharing the rest of this brokenness now after all we've recovered from?"

In her southern, no-doubt-about-it charm, she simply replied, "I don't know, but if God is asking you to do it, there is a good reason. Let me know when you decide to talk to Todd so I can be praying for you."

Driving home from lunch, I was much less certain about my ability to have that conversation with Todd than Marianne was but God now had my attention.

∽

Over the next several weeks, I had many tearful prayer conversations with God about what I felt he was now asking of me. Though nothing I felt prompted to share with Todd was as devastating as what we'd endured the past year, it was all premarital stuff that happened when we were broken up; I was still terrified the revelations would do harm to the progress we'd made in our relationship. Ultimately, however, what turned the tide for me was my relationship with Jesus. He had become my best friend over that last year, and I trusted him. As he was calling me deeper into relationship and ministry, I knew the enemy would always use my past to accuse me, and I knew I could never live that way. If I was going to be all in with God, I had to be all in, regardless of the cost.

After much resignation, the night finally came when I surrendered and was ready to share all of the things from my past that were left hidden with Todd. I tried to be as prepared as possible, writing out what I wanted to say so I wouldn't forget anything, enlisting a few good friends to pray for us and arranging for the kids to sleepover with friends. Still, I wasn't prepared for how the evening would unfold.

Sitting on the couch, I reached over to hold Todd's hand before giving my reasoning for what I was about to share. Tenderly and carefully, I began, "I feel like the Holy Spirit has been prompting me for weeks now to share some things from my past that you don't know. I honestly don't want to share them, and I'm so afraid you are going to hate me, but I feel like God wants me to get the rest of this out in the open, so there is nothing that can come back and hijack our marriage or what God may have for us in the future."

With little emotion, he nodded and replied, "Okay."

And so, I began to read from my paper about the final bits and pieces of brokenness that had been left hidden, wreaking havoc in my soul—a one-night stand, drunkenness, and the shame surrounding it all. When I finished, tears filled Todd's eyes, and he squeezed my hand as he spoke, "I love you, and I forgive you. I know that's not who you are anymore." With that, we embraced and I immediately felt like a thousand-pound boulder had been released from my chest. "Thank you, Jesus," I whispered in silent prayer as we hugged, feeling so grateful for Todd's response and for God's strength to be obedient and share even though I'd been terrified to do so.

It was late at this point, so after exchanging a few more words, I got up to get ready for bed. Having washed my face and put on my PJs, I climbed into bed, figuring Todd would join me soon. After an hour of waiting, still no Todd. My mind quickly began to narrate, "See he's angry about what you told him. He's not really okay with it." I leaned into these thoughts for a few moments but then decided it was smarter to just go get answers than write a story in my mind, and I went to find him.

Walking down the hall, I entered the living room, but he was no longer there. I could see the light on in the front office, and when I approached, I saw him sitting at the desk in front of the computer, reading what looked like a letter. Sensing my presence, he quickly closed the screen, clearly hiding something from me. Nervously, he said, "I'll be right there."

I was anxious to know what he was reading and decided to just wait and ask him when he finally came to bed. To my surprise, when he walked into the bedroom, he was carrying a letter. Holding it up and giving it a wave, he spoke, "This is what was on the screen. I was just finishing it so I could give it to you." Climbing into bed next to me, he elaborated nervously, "It's funny, all this time that God's been prompting you to share these last hidden things from your past, he's been prompting me to do the same." Tears began to well up in his eyes now as he continued, "These things are gonna be really hard for you to read, and I wanted to tell you a year ago, but Pastor John said you weren't strong enough to hear them back then, that telling you would have completely ruined any chance we had of healing, so I waited."

Trembling, I took the letter from his hand, in no way prepared for what I was about to read. "Before you read," he continued "I want you to know that Mike and Kim also know what is in this letter, and they are praying for you as you read it. Kim says she'll be available if you need to talk or process later and to let you know she loves you."

I had no idea what to expect, but as I began to read, tears filled my eyes and a familiar pain began to creep into my chest. A one-night stand with someone different, prior to the affair with Ashley. The heaviness in my chest began to throb, and my head began to spin. Immediately, I dropped the letter and ran to the bathroom to throw up. Leaning back, I flushed the toilet and wiped my mouth with a Kleenex before sinking to the floor, laying my cheek on the cool floor tile. What a familiar spot this place on the bathroom floor was becoming to wrestle with God about Todd.

A few moments later, Todd cautiously peeked around the door into the bathroom, whispering, "Can I come in?"

Slowly, I sat up, crisscrossing my legs as I leaned back against the wall. "Sure," I said with a nod.

Coming in, he sat on the floor next to me. "Do you hate me?" he whispered through tears.

Tears began to flow in torrents down my face as I tried to talk through my clenched throat and the lump that had now formed, "I want to. Everything in me wants to hate you right now, but I also know you are not that guy anymore. I don't know what to do."

For a long time, we just sat there, saying nothing.

Finally, I believe only through the grace of Jesus, I broke the silence, knowing what we had to do. The past year had changed us both in profound ways. So reaching over, I grabbed Todd's hand as I spoke, "Pray with me now. We need to pray together now that God protect our hearts from hating each other and from destroying what he's been rebuilding in us. Because I am so afraid at this moment of hating you again."

Turning toward one another, we grasped hands and leaned in, our foreheads touching as the tears flowed. The prayer was raw and simple, "Lord, help us."

❧

The next few weeks were brutal as I tried to reconcile what I knew about the man who was now my husband with the one who had done such harm to my heart in the past. Whatever my mind might tell me, whatever I knew about the old Todd was gone and the man with whom I now did life was different. This Todd loved Jesus, our kids, and me. This Todd was willing to admit his faults and failures, seek forgiveness, and fight for the good of our family. This Todd, as was I, was not willing to let anything remain hidden in our relationship and was willing to trust God's healing hand when he shared. If God was orchestrating all of this, could I not trust it?

There were no easy answers to the questions and the pain that had resurfaced, but true to his nature, God drew close as I sought his counsel. Daily he would remind me of just how far he had brought us over the past year and of the dreams he had been placing in my heart. I could choose to believe what I knew was true or I could lean into distressing questions my mind brought, "Was this past year all for nothing? Had God really brought us this far to let us now fall apart?"

As I wrestled with my thoughts and questions, God brought me to Psalm 55 (NIV).

> Listen to my prayer, O God,
> do not ignore my plea;
> hear me and answer me.
> My thoughts trouble me and I am distraught
> because of what my enemy is saying,
> because of the threats of the wicked;
> for they bring down suffering on me
> and assail me in their anger.
> My heart is in anguish within me;

the terrors of death have fallen on me.
Fear and trembling have beset me;
horror has overwhelmed me.
I said, "Oh, that I had the wings of a dove!
I would fly away and be at rest.
I would flee far away
and stay in the desert;
I would hurry to my place of shelter,
far from the tempest and storm."
Lord, confuse the wicked, confound their words,
for I see violence and strife in the city.
Day and night they prowl about on its walls;
malice and abuse are within it.
Destructive forces are at work in the city;
threats and lies never leave its streets.
If an enemy were insulting me,
I could endure it;
if a foe were rising against me,
I could hide.
But it is you, a man like myself,
my companion, my close friend,
with whom I once enjoyed sweet fellowship
at the house of God,
as we walked about
among the worshipers.
Let death take my enemies by surprise;
let them go down alive to the realm of the dead,
for evil finds lodging among them.
As for me, I call to God,
and the Lord saves me.
Evening, morning and noon
I cry out in distress,
and he hears my voice.
He rescues me unharmed
from the battle waged against me,
even though many oppose me.

God, who is enthroned from of old,
who does not change—
he will hear them and humble them,
because they have no fear of God.
My companion attacks his friends;
he violates his covenant.
His talk is smooth as butter,
yet war is in his heart;
his words are more soothing than oil,
yet they are drawn swords.
Cast your cares on the Lord
and he will sustain you;
he will never let
the righteous be shaken.
But you, God, will bring down the wicked
into the pit of decay;
the bloodthirsty and deceitful
will not live out half their days.
But as for me, I trust in you.

There was such comfort in reading the words of anguish from King David and how he sought the Lord in the midst of his pain and betrayal. I was grateful to know this kind of expression was okay; and it brought hope, strength, and courage to cling to God and to what I now knew to be true of Todd. These words gave me the resilience I needed to keep moving forward in the hopes that one day we would be fully restored as a couple and a willingness to trust God in the slowness of our healing journey.

Though it felt so mean and unnecessary at the moment, God's timing had been perfect. He knew these revelations would be incredibly difficult for both of us, but he also knew they were necessary to release us into the future he was preparing. He had been strengthening both of our hearts over the past year to be ready to hear his request to reveal the hidden past, to share when prompted, to receive what we heard from one another with grace and forgiveness, and he had provided the necessary love and support we would need to champion us through these new revelations.

God loved us too much to allow our past brokenness to have power over our future and so in his grace, with our willingness, he unearthed it and in time brought healing.

ॐ

This part of my story could easily have been left out of the book and God would still be honored. However, the reason I included it is to show the extreme lengths God will go to not just fix what is broken in our lives but to bring about complete healing. God is not interested in wound care or what I call a "Jesus Band-Aid." His desire is complete restoration, but we must be willing to work with him in the process. Though it is costly, it is worth it to live without fear of the past coming back to do harm.

Todd or I could have chosen to keep these parts of our past hidden from one another and I do believe God would have still loved us and continued to do life with us. However, he knew far better than us at the time just how real, witty, and extremely cunning the enemy can be with hidden things. If there were even hints of things in our past to fear, he would absolutely use them against us. This cloud of fear was not something God wanted us to live under.

God also knew, well before I did, how he wanted to use our story in the future. As he began preparing me to write it and share it openly, he knew the enemy would use whatever means possible to keep me distanced from Todd, who would become my biggest supporter and champion in what was to come. So in his grace, God led me to another Daniel 3 moment; this time, inviting both Todd and I to a final step of surrender, into the "fiery furnace" once again with him. As we both willingly entered in, trusting whatever may come, he dug up all the roots from both our pasts, all things that bound and shackled us, and Jesus walked with us in the flames of our brokenness as we worked toward healing.

Eventually, God would call us out of the fire, bringing profound healing through these final revelations of the past, only allowing the flames to refine, not destroy. When we finally emerged, we no longer smelled like the smoky pain of our past. Todd would no longer live in shame for what he had done, and I would no longer live without trusting him. Now released from what previously bound us, God then tethered the two of us together in Christ, a strong cord of three, with a story of redemption that others could hold onto as they sought this God who we would one day openly proclaim through our story.

Part 3

EVERYTHING REDEEMED

I have swept away your offenses like a cloud,
your sins like the morning mist.
Return to me, for I have redeemed you.

—Isaiah 44:22 (NIV)

Let the redeemed of the Lord tell their story—
those he redeemed from the hand of the foe.

—Psalms 107:2 (NIV)

14

A New Way of Life

Our brokenness opened us up to
a deeper way of sharing
our lives and offering each other hope.

—Henri J. M. Nouwen,
Life of the Beloved

Kintsugi has captured my attention in recent years. It is a strikingly beautiful, traditional form of Japanese art that uses precious metals such as liquid gold and liquid silver to bind broken pieces of pottery back together while at the same time enhancing the break itself. This exquisite work is known as the Art of Precious Scars. Every piece is absolutely unique because of the randomness by which it is shattered, and the "scars" from where it has been rebuilt now become the piece's most gorgeous focal point. In many ways, each piece becomes far more beautiful than it ever was before broken, but even more impressive than its beauty is the strength and stability each piece now possesses.

When I was initially introduced to Kintsugi, each piece I saw mesmerized me. The lines, the broken pieces, the thickness and thinness of the metal in various places, and the intricate time and care needed to reconstruct each piece was gripping. Allured by each design, surprising thoughts and questions began to arise within me. "If God can bring this kind of beauty to a broken piece of pottery, how much more can he do with a broken life that allows Jesus to move in and fill all their broken places with his glory? What kind of beauty and strength might God bring to a life that allowed him, the master creator, to put all the broken pieces back together with the precious blood of his son?" This was the mystery of the Gospel that I'd already come to know through my own story, but now with powerful imagery in which to share it.

In this next season of life, Todd and I did not yet know that our brokenness and scars could be beautiful or that they might be a focal point to draw others to God. We certainly did not feel stronger or reinforced by the broken parts of our story. In fact, I'd say we still felt very fragile as our broken pieces were still "curing" at this point. However, we did know we were moving forward and trusted that God was redeeming all our past brokenness. It was with this knowledge that we chose to move into a new way of life, being open about our story and God's capacity to redeem…everything.

ॐ

Showing those around us God's power to redeem would not begin with us sharing the ugly parts of our story. It would begin simply with a celebration. A wedding.

More than a year had passed since the revelation of the affair, the evening Todd met me in the bedroom of our Texas home with a request. "Close your eyes and give me your hand. I have a surprise for you," he said with excitement.

"Okay," I said with a huge childlike grin, closing my eyes and slipping my left hand into his. Before me, he walked, slowly guiding me down the long hallway into the living room. It was late, and the kids were already fast asleep, so the house was completely quiet. Maneuvering me around the couch and in front of the coffee table, he gently seated me on the far-left cushion closest to the fireplace, which I could feel emanating heat toward me. "Okay, open your eyes," he whispered.

The room was completely dark, except for the light glowing from the flames. As my eyes adjusted, there in front of the fireplace, I saw a plate full of chocolate-covered strawberries, one of my favorite treats. My heart swelled as I looked up at Todd standing close. "Happy Valentine's Day," he said warmly. Then, slowly he moved forward, picking up the plate of strawberries and kneeling down to present them to me as he said, "Go ahead, have one."

Peering over the plate, my eyes darted back and forth looking for the biggest one when I noticed something slightly out of place. There in the middle of the mound of strawberries sat a tiny basket, no more than an inch in diameter, filled with salt. Nestled in the white grains sat a small gold band. Quickly my eyes moved up to meet Todd's gaze, his eyes now filled with tears. Sitting the plate down, he grabbed the ring from the little basket, holding it up as he spoke, "Would you marry me now that I am a Christian man?"

No words came as my throat tightened and tears flooded my eyes, but holding out my left hand, I nodded in agreement. Slipping the ring onto my finger, snug, up close to my original wedding band, Todd leaned in to hug me, whispering tenderly, "I love you so much."

In his embrace the tension released and my words finally came, "I love you too. And of course, I will marry you."

✎

Hearing grand stories of redemption and life change breed skepticism in many people and, truthfully, for good reason. I think everyone has encountered someone who has "supposedly" changed, only to find out they are the same old person they'd always been. While I understand the hesitancy to believe, faith requires us to be open to God's power of redemption. The caveat is to not check our brains at the door. God gave us wisdom and insight as human beings and expects us to use them, to pay attention and discern if someone's behavior is truly genuine.

While I personally had witnessed more than enough consistency in Todd's behavior to trust his changes were real, some friends and family from back home were not so easily convinced. Even without knowledge of the affair, there were those who had experienced Todd's unhappiness over the years and who simply were not thrilled that the kids and I had moved a thousand miles away with him. Which is why we chose a wedding as the catalyst to reveal the changes our entire family had undergone the past year.

Reactions were mixed by those who received the invitation to our remarriage ceremony scheduled for May 30, 2003, in Texas, that stated we were entering into a "New Beginning in Christ." Most people, without true knowledge of how bad our marriage had been, were perplexed as to why we were doing it but congratulatory, assuming we had just turned into religious fanatics. For those who knew what had happened, the reactions were even further mixed. Some thought it was a great idea, some thought it was unnecessary, and some were very forthcoming about their hesitations.

I remember the conversation with one family member who flat out told me, "Steph, he hasn't changed, he's only saying what you want to hear so he doesn't lose his family." These were hard words to hear, but I knew the backstory of this person and understood why they would be skeptical. I would not let their pain influence my reply, so I held fast to my belief in the changes I had witnessed, saying, "I appreciate your concern, but Todd *is* different, and you should come see for yourself."

Then there were those friends in Texas who had become like family. Some knew our story and some didn't, but regardless, they all wanted to celebrate our decision to live as a family dedicated to living out our faith in Jesus. It was shaping up to be quite a day, filled with believers, nonbelievers, champions of Todd and skeptics alike, but still, we were excited.

The feeling of butterflies filled my stomach as I stood in the lobby of our church, making last minute adjustments to Sydney's hair and Cody's little tie. The kids looked so precious. Sydney was glowing in a shiny, periwinkle blue dress, her hair pulled back from her face with little silver clips crowning the top of her head and holding a white wicker basket with ribbons flowing from its handle. And Cody appeared so dapper in his periwinkle blue dress shirt, navy vest and tie, looking like a miniature version of his dad. My dress was simple, just a cream-colored, off-the-rack dress from Ross Dress For Less, but it was perfect for the day, and I felt beautiful. Now that we were all ready, it was time to begin.

Out the front doors into the glorious Texas sunshine, the three of us walked together across the parking lot. Nearing the edge of the grass, leading into the canopy of hundred-foot tall Texas pine trees, I could hear instrumental music beginning to play. Bending down to eye level, I looked at both kids as I spoke, "You guys ready to do this?" A smile and a nod from Cody followed by an exuberant "Yes!" from Sydney affirmed me, so one by one we each began our entrance.

Friends had transformed the wooded area out in front of the church into a simple outdoor chapel. Folding chairs on two sides created an aisle that led to a small platform stage where Todd, I, and Pastor John could stand, with a backdrop of flowers and tulle to accent us. Additionally, off to the front left was a small table where we could take communion together as part of the ceremony. It was perfect.

Cody led the way, followed by Sydney dropping little white flower petals, and I then made my entrance. Walking slowly, I tried to take in every face of the forty friends and family who had come to support us before making eye contact with Todd. There he stood on the platform, in his suit and tie, arms slightly crossed in front, holding his left wrist with his right hand. He looked so nervous, but handsome as always, even with tears streaming down his cheeks. When our gaze met, my heart quickened as I remembered the words of Pastor Larry only fifteen months earlier at our first counseling session, "Steph, you can heal from this. And if God gets a hold of Todd's heart, not only will he save your marriage, but you may just get the husband you've always dreamed of." Never in a million years could I have believed such a story of redemption was possible, and yet there I was with the husband I never would have dared to believe could exist.

Finally making my way down front, I turned to give Sydney my flowers before taking Todd's hand to help me up on the platform. The ceremony was short and sweet with Pastor John relaying words on the significance of marriage and God's power to redeem, Todd and I sharing new vows, and us taking communion together. Steven Curtis Chapman's song "I Will Be Here" played in the background as Todd and I took the bread and the wine and then grasping hands and touching foreheads as we prayed together before closing the ceremony. This element of communion and prayer had not been present in our original wedding, but this day, we were acknowledging our faith before those watching and the fact that more than simply being married, we were choosing to enter into a covenant of marriage with one another and with God. From this day forward, there was no turning back.

Faithful to their amazing generosity and hospitality, the day ended with a celebration at Mark and Belinda's house. It was an evening full of fun, laughter, good food, great friends, and family who'd made the journey to celebrate all God had done for our family. While not everyone knew all the details leading up to the day or understood our faith journey, there was no doubting how much love for each other and Jesus now filled our new way of life.

In the weeks and months to come, when appropriate, we would share more about the brokenness that had plagued our marriage with friends and family. The responses, especially from family, were beautifully representative of God's transformative power. From my sister came the proclamation, "Well, if God can save Todd, I'm pretty sure he can save anyone!"

And from my stepfather Dale, the affirmation, "Steph, you can't fake the kind of changes we see in Todd." The knowledge of God's power to redeem was beginning to leak out to those around us, and we couldn't be happier. What once had been shattered was now becoming a thing of strength and beauty.

It would be more than ten years before we would share the details of our story with the kids and the significance of what really took place under the Texas pines that day. Regardless, at the time, they still knew something was different about our family. Sydney specifically at the tender age of nine could tell you, "There was a day when Daddy knew Jesus and when he didn't and now he's different." Only God.

⁍

Some reading may now wonder, "Is life with God really this simple?" If that is you, let me lovingly say, "Please go back and reread the first two sections because you've missed something." None of the choices leading up to our new way of living were easy or without struggle and moving forward would require continuous surrender and trust in God and one another. The wedding was simply a gift God gave us as a memorial of how far we'd come and a stake in the ground moment to cling to when life got hard again.

To forgive and forget is a beautiful part of God's character, but it is in no way spoken of in Scripture as something human beings are expected to do; I've checked. In fact, I would argue that if God wanted us to "forget" when we forgive, he would not have wired our brains with such an amazing capacity to remember things. The truth is, remembering once we've forgiven is not so we can punish or hold something over someone's head. Rather, it is a means by which we can evaluate, when appropriate, the ability for restoration in a relationship. Contrary to what some believe, forgiveness does not always mean the restoring of a relationship. We can forgive someone, and they still will not be safe to have in our lives.

Todd and I had forgiven much, and we were moving forward, a new beginning in Christ, but we were still human with brains that remembered the past. Over the coming years, alarm bells would go off in my head if something felt even remotely similar to past events. When this happened, I would not hide my fears from Todd but talk openly with him, not to throw the past in his face but to keep healing present in our future. For Todd, there were similar things that would trigger feelings of shame or remorse; these, too, we would talk through. Every conversation leading to a deeper level of trust and intimacy, every conversation, an opportunity for us to live out our forgiveness and new way of life.

The choice to continually fight for love and our family was so very different from the world's view of "get out of the marriage if you're not happy." We had witnessed God show up in the fight and now on the backside began to experience the joy of restoration. Much to our surprise, our restored brokenness was making us alluring to those watching. The wedding had revealed our story of redemption and transformation, and now God would begin to call us even deeper into his story.

15

It's Time

*But note that God is both our refuge and
strength. We don't run to Him to hide;
we run to Him for help. He hides us that He
might help us, and then he thrusts us back
into the battle that we might accomplish His
will in the world. God does not hide us to
pamper us, but to prepare us. He
strengthens us that He might use us.*

—Warren W. Wiersbe,
The Bumps Are What You Climb On

*The desire to hide from life, trouble, pain, and even God is such an instinc-
tual part of the human condition. Adam and Eve tried to hide themselves
from God in the garden after they'd eaten the forbidden fruit. Moses ran to
hide himself in the desert after killing the Egyptian. King David hid from
his duty of going off to war which led to his indiscretion with Bathsheba.
And the prophet Elijah ran for his life to hide in the wilderness from the
wicked Queen Jezebel. All these major protagonists in God's story chose
hiding as a way to cope with the events unfolding in their lives. These five
names only scratch the surface of the long list of people who also did the
same in Scripture and who continue to do so in our world today. The writer
of Ecclesiastes was correct, "What has been will be again, what has been*

done will be done again; there is nothing new under the sun" (Eccles. 1:9 NIV). Hiding is in our nature.

There is, however, a form of hiding in God when trouble hits that is very different than hiding from God. It is the imagery we see in Scripture of a mother hen gathering her chicks beneath the shelter of her wings to guide and protect them as they grow. It is a tender image given to reveal God's heart to us as his children. If we allow him, in seasons of pain and trouble, he will draw us close, nestling us into his breast, near his heart, hiding us in his love while we heal and find hope to once again engage life. It is a place of warmth, safety, and protection, but is not a place we can stay forever. Only he knows when we will be ready, but when we are, like any good mother hen, God will send us out from under the covering of his wings. He will still be with us and fight to protect us when necessary, but he knows when it's time for us to take our place in the world again.

Several years had passed since God led us to Texas, the place he had chosen for us to hide in him as we healed. Truly, it was a haven where he enveloped us in his love, safety, protection, and healing. There he strengthened us and taught us how to individually follow him but also how to be a family once again. Now that we were strong, the Spirit would come with new, surprising nudges toward the future God had for us, requiring (as was becoming normal) more surrender. This time we were ready…kind of.

There was nothing not to love about our life in Texas. After nearly three years, much of life had finally come together. We had reestablished our financial situation as Todd continued to work in his field of expertise and I worked part-time at a local printing company doing graphic design. The kids were thriving at school, extracurricular activities, and building great friendships. Todd and I were doing fantastic as a couple. Spiritually, we were growing as a family. We had wonderful friends and a great church home. And as a bonus, we got to do it all in the gorgeous Texas sunshine.

We are warm-weather people, so the hotter and more humid, the better; the Houston area did not disappoint. Every chance we could get, we were out in nature, exploring God's creation with the kids on hikes, bike rides, or simple walks through the neighborhood. Our favorite moments were those near the coast. Though it's not the most beautiful beach, living within ninety minutes of Galveston was a treat as well as all the bay areas in between. It's hard to be "blah" enjoying a fifty-degree Thanksgiving walking along the beach, definitely not as warm as we like, but still good! We were genuinely the happiest we had ever been up to that point in life and living in Texas was a significant part of the equation.

Now that stability had come, lots of questions began to stir in me about the future. Life had been difficult and chaotic for so long to just be happy and enjoy life felt very unfamiliar. Chaos can easily become a dysfunctional but familiar friend that we embrace if we are not careful. So I began to wonder what I was to do with myself now that I no longer lived in a constant state of worry about my marriage and family? Dare I begin to open my heart up to new endeavors?

With no idea what may possibly lay ahead, I decided to begin seeking God's direction for the future. Maybe he could have something to say about what came next?

Graphic design had been the career path I'd been on for nearly fifteen years. In high school, I was blessed to be part of a trade school opportunity my junior and senior year that opened the door for a pretty decent job after graduation. While I enjoyed the creativity and found myself skilled at it, there was never passion or a sense of purpose attached to it. At eighteen years of age, it was simply a direction to take and a good income. Now that I was a bit older and stable, I longed for a job that was more than a paycheck.

As I prayed about what was next, I also reached out to the amazing mentors and friends God had placed in my life for wisdom and counsel. None of them tried to tell me what to do but wholeheartedly agreed to come alongside me in prayer as I sought God's direction. In doing so, a theme began to emerge in our conversations...ministry.

I remember shaking my head in disbelief as one of the older mentors I did life with said, "Steph, maybe God is calling you into ministry?" Graciously, I smiled, offering a "Who knows, maybe?" reply, while deep inside feeling very unworthy of such a calling. Yes, I was enjoying teaching Bible studies and the mission work I had gotten to engage in the previous year, but could God really use someone like me, with my jacked-up past in a paid ministry role? I was doubtful.

Over the next several months, God continued to place this idea before me in various ways through books, sermons, conversations, radio broadcast, etc., until it was undeniable that ministry was something he was nudging me to consider. Even more specifically, sharing our story in some capacity kept coming up.

I was so nervous the day I brought this up to Todd. For months, I had kept it to myself, wanting to be sure this was indeed God's nudge, but now that I was certain, it was time. Todd had come into the kitchen to grab a drink and rest after doing some work around the house. As he sat down at the kitchen table, I joined him, asking, "Hey, can we talk for a sec?"

"Sure, what's up?" he said.

Confidently, I began, "Well, I've been feeling for a while like God may be calling me into ministry."

Though I didn't recognize it at the time, this moment marked the beginning of Todd becoming my biggest cheerleader in ministry, as he responded with a nod, "Yeah, I can see that."

I continued, "Well, I'd like to explore the local Christian college and the possibility of going back to school for ministry; if we can afford it?"

"Sure. I think that is a good next step," he replied.

So far, so good, but I was scared about sharing the final detail. Slowly I began, "And...I think...what is to be part of my future ministry endeavors is me sharing our story."

Without thought or hesitation, he quickly replied, "Okay."

In surprise, I asked, "Really? You are okay with this?"

Again, no hesitation as he simply responded, "Yeah, I'm okay with it."

"Well, you know, even within the walls of the church, some people will judge you for your part of the story. I mean, I know I don't come across all that great either earlier in our dating relationship, but as a husband who cheated, people may judge you," I said, wanting to be sure that he really understood what I was proposing.

Next, with such a wonderfully childlike faith in God's purposes, Todd confidently replied, "Well, I don't know much and I'm still new to all this faith stuff, but what I do know is this. If someone wants to judge me for the things that I did before I knew Jesus, then I'm pretty sure that is their issue to deal with God on, not mine."

He then looked deeply into my eyes and with a smile said, "Tell our story. I support you 100 percent."

Everyone in my circle of friends was delighted to hear I was moving toward a career path in ministry and was very supportive in the daunting process to come. Days turned into weeks and weeks into months as I entered into the world of college enrollment. All down time outside of work and the kids were filled with my college application, entrance exam prep, essays, letters of recommendation, scholarship applications, and student loan research. It was an exciting process, and I was grateful to begin embarking on such a journey with God, but as sure as I was of the call to ministry, something felt off in my spirit about entering into school in Houston.

As I talked regularly to God about my hesitation with the Houston school, I found my mind inevitably would be drawn to thoughts of Missouri and our family back there. It was consistent enough that I started to ask the question when praying, "Lord, what's that all about?" No answer directly came, but I continued to take notice and pray about it for several weeks.

Finally, the day came when all the details required for school were securely in place. All that was needed was for me to enroll in summer classes and the journey would begin. The problem was, I couldn't get myself to do it. All I knew in my gut was that something wasn't right.

The next day, I found myself at the kitchen table once again with Todd. We weren't talking about anything heavy, just life—the kids, how the grass in the backyard was growing, what to eat for dinner, etc., when I felt the nudge in my spirit, seemingly out of nowhere, to say exactly what came to mind. Reaching across the table, I grabbed Todd's hand and very solemnly began to say what I had been denying to myself the past few weeks, "I think…"

Todd interrupted me with the same solemn look on his face and completed my sentence, "It's time to move back."

Shaking my head in agreement, tears began to fill my eyes as I spoke, "Yeah. I think God is saying it's time to go back to Missouri."

Much like before when God had been prompting Todd and I to share the hidden parts of our story, God was nudging both of us, unknown to each other, that it was time to move back to Missouri. In the years to come, this would become a common practice in the way God would lead us, knitting both of our hearts together in complete unity before calling us to new endeavors both great and small. For this season, the nudge was to return to Missouri, and though we would miss Texas terribly, we would go if that was what God wanted us to do.

Several weeks of prayer and conversation accompanied our kitchen table realization to return to Missouri, and when we finally had a rough timeline in place, we began making phone calls to family back home about our imminent return. Everyone was excited, none more than the grandparents ready to have Syd and Cody close once again. It was nice to feel so wanted, but leaving behind the life we had built in Texas would prove to be harder than we ever expected.

The first difficult task would be to share our decision with the community of friends we had built. Everyone was saddened to hear our news but supportive of our being obedient to God's next move in our lives. Interestingly, as our time in the Houston area was coming to an end, so was the time of other supports God has placed around us. Mike and Kim were departing for his next military assignment, leaving within weeks of our move. The women's ministry mentor at my church who'd poured so much into me was moving on, and within the next year, Pastor John who'd mentored Todd so closely would take a new assignment as well. It was as if God had assembled this band of people around us for this special season of healing and then dispersed us all when his work was complete.

Finding a job for Todd would be the next task. In the big scheme of things, this was not something we were overly concerned about. Todd is a hard worker with an impressive resume in his industry, and moving in the summer months would make it easy to find work. The only issue would be questions surrounding why he was not returning to his old company. New employers would definitely want to know why he wouldn't want to go back to a company with whom he had spent ten years. Thankfully, God gave us favor as his old company owner was willing to give Todd a great reference and acknowledge there simply wasn't a place for him there at this time.

The next big hurdle was the kids and the upcoming school year. It was very important to us, in the midst of such change, for the kids to start their news schools at the beginning of the year with everyone else. Syd was starting middle school, and this made it even more important as this can be a critical age for connection and acceptance with peers. The problem was the housing market in Texas was not great at the time, and there was little interest in our home once we'd put it up for sale.

This was one of those crucial moments when Todd and I, as a couple, began to learn the power of discernment. What were we to do with this wrench thrown into our plans? Was the house not selling evidence that God was saying don't go back? Was this the enemy trying to hijack God's plans for us? Or was this simply a bad housing market forcing us to decide if we would follow God's plan even if the details weren't coming together as we thought? Would we trust what God had already nudged us toward even if it was hard?

God's nudges had been too clear about returning to Missouri, so regardless of what happened with the house, we decided to stay the course and move. Todd's parents were generous enough to allow us to live with them so the kids could start school on time as we waited for our home in Texas to sell. And so, in July 2005, exactly three years after we'd arrived, we packed up another U-Haul truck and began our journey back to the place that had been the backdrop for our lives being shattered.

ॐ

How does one even begin to say goodbye to a place that has brought such profound healing? Yes, we loved the Texas sunshine and the community of friends we had built, but it was so much more than that. Whenever a person says goodbye to something, there is the loss itself, but then there are "the million little paper cuts" that inflict so much pain. These are the small things, the things no one else sees or knows about, but that you miss so dearly and that cause your heart to ache.

The local Christian radio station in Houston was 89.3 KSBJ and their tagline was "God listens." Yes, in Texas, it felt like God was listening to our cries for help. Quite unexpectedly, the music and encouragement of this radio station had become a daily part of my life in Texas, and I couldn't imagine not having it. Apps and online streaming were not a thing yet, and the area we were moving back to had no such station yet. How would that part of my life change, and where would I now find that joy?

Then there was our favorite restaurant Taco Cabana, Cody's special doughnut shop with the "pink donies" he loved, the Hispanic grocery store I'd come to appreciate shopping at, and the palm tree we had planted in the front yard that I longed to watch grow. The little things with God in Texas are what had come to make up the substance of our new life in him and now we were leaving all the people and things that had taught us to live and love with such intensity. How could we go? How could we leave this life we had built behind?

The answer we sought to help us move forward would come through a familiar passage of Scripture. In the book of Joshua is recorded the story of the nation of Israel finally moving in to possess the land God had promised to them forty years earlier when they'd left Egyptian slavery. In Joshua chapters 3 and 4, as Israel crossed over the Jordan River that God had parted for them on dry ground; Joshua called together twelve men, one from each tribe and told each one to take a stone from the middle of the Jordan riverbed before crossing over. He then tells them, "These stones are to be a memorial to the people of Israel forever" (Josh. 4:7 NIV). Joshua then, once everyone had crossed, sets the stones up as a memorial to remind the Israelites of how God had parted the waters for them and as a way to share with future generations all that God had done for the nation of Israel.

Remembering, yes, remembering and sharing all that God had done to restore our family would be how we would find the strength to move. And so, before we left, off to Home Depot I went to purchase a two-by-two-foot terracotta stone in the shape of Texas. Wherever we would land in the future, this stone would be placed in our front yard landscaping, as a memorial of all the ways God had brought healing to our family in Texas.

The two-day journey from Texas to Missouri with our entire life once again in a truck was in no way adequate to grieve what we were leaving or to prepare us for what lay ahead. But one thing we knew for certain: the same God who had called us to Texas, who had hidden us and redeemed our story there, was the same God going with us back to Missouri. As he was with us in Texas, he would be with us in Missouri. He had redeemed our marriage and family, now he would begin to redeem the place where so much hurt had started. Back in Missouri, he would teach us how to live out our faith before family and friends who only knew the old broken parts of our story. There would be no more hiding. Now it was finally time for us to take our place back in the state that had previously wounded us and to point others to the God who we now knew could redeem anything and everything.

16

Call Back

The mountain climbing of life is
serious, but glorious, business;
it takes strength and steadiness to reach the summit.
And as our view becomes better as we
gain altitude, and as we discover
things of importance, we should "call
back" our encouragement to others.

—L. B. Cowman,
Streams in the Desert

It's been more than twenty years since that blustery February morning when I found myself sitting all alone with Jesus in the Burger King parking lot next to my house; my life shattered. So much has transpired since that day, good and bad, just a fraction of which I've tried to capture in these pages. My mind muses as I come to this place of wrapping up, "Have I said enough? Have I honored Jesus thoroughly with my words and our story? Will you, the reader, see my Savior and his power to redeem—everything? Is there anything I may have missed that would be important for you to know?"

Sitting here, staring out the window, pondering these questions, one last thought comes to mind. "Why? Why would I write any of this down and allow you to peek into these most intimate, painful, details of my story? What do I gain from laying the brokenness of my past before you? What motivation could possibly be strong enough to warrant such vulnerability?"

The answer is twofold.

First, and most likely unsurprising at this point, is because I believe God asked me to write it. I always try my best to follow through with requests from my Lord, though I honestly drag my feet at times. For nearly seventeen years, the Holy Spirit has been nudging me to write our story, and though I've shared it from a stage or in person countless times, finally, in this season of life, I was ready to actually write it. Sharing our story is first and foremost, for God's glory. It is my "hallelujah," my praise to him for all he has done in my life. I have nothing else to give him, and so this book has become my offering. Oh, how I hope he is pleased with it.

The second reason, possibly a little unexpected, is…you. I want you to know there is a God who sees you and who pursues you to the very end. I want you to know there is a God who loves you and who wants to redeem, through his son Jesus, all the brokenness in your life—everything. I want you to know there is a God who strategically places people in your life, maybe even through a simple book, to "call back" to you and encourage you that he has not abandoned you and that he is still with you in whatever circumstance you may find yourself today. I have tried to paint an authentic picture for you of what God's redemption has looked like in my life. It was not quick, simple, or easy, but God was there for me, and I believe he wants to be there for you too.

৯

If you were to spend time with Todd and I today, you would never know about the fiery trial we went through in our marriage unless I told you. Todd does not walk around under a cloud of shame. I do not distrust him at all or hate men in general. There are no lingering jabs from our past that we thrust upon one another when we argue (yes, we still argue sometimes). We simply seem to have a good life and come across as a couple who are truly best friends, have been married for twenty-nine years, raised two children, and who love Jesus. We are not faking our happiness or trying to hide the past; it's just not lingering in our day-to-day life anymore. This, however, is ultimately why I share our story.

Some of my greatest sadness comes from the way many Christ-followers, especially leaders and pastors, bury their backstories of redemption. No, not everyone needs to know all the details of a life like I've set before you in this book, but we have to say more than "God saved me."

"Saved you from what?" is always my first thought—not to get the "dirt" on their life, but to glean an understanding of yet another picture of God's power to redeem. When we set before the watching world a view of the Christian life that is perfect and without struggle, we are lying and denying the grace extended to us through the faith we possess. This also, quite unintentionally, sets before those seeking Jesus and those trying to live faithfully for him, a standard they feel is impossible to achieve. Thus, it is imperative that we who follow Jesus learn to live out our faith with authenticity about our past and vulnerability in our present.

Whenever I share about our past, I always do so in tandem with the story from Daniel 3 of the "fiery furnace" which I've referenced twice in our story already because it has so many layers that are applicable to my journey. When you read the story of Shadrach, Meshach, and Abednego, it appears that they were thrown into the fiery furnace against their will by an evil king on an ego trip. While this is absolutely true, there is also the truth present that this whole situation could have been avoided had the young Hebrews simply bowed down to worship the image of gold the king had erected. They could have still loved God and taken the path of least resistance, but their faith would not allow them to yield to the threat before them. Instead, they chose faithfulness to God, and in doing so, he literally met them in the midst of their fiery trial.

Scripture tells us that though the three young men had been firmly bound prior to being thrown in the furnace, what the king witnessed was four men, walking around in the flames unbound and unharmed. This fourth man is believed to be what is known as a "theophany," a physical manifestation of God in the Old Testament.

As he walked with the young men in the flames, he protected them, ultimately rendering them unharmed. But even more true to his faithfulness, when the young men finally emerged from the furnace, we are told, "They saw that the fire had not harmed their bodies, nor was a hair of their heads singed; their robes were not scorched, and there was no smell of fire on them" (Dan. 3:27 NIV). Amazing!

Ultimately, there was no evidence on these young men of having been in the flames, except a deeper knowledge of the God who walked with them in the fire. While these young men were not physically harmed, I think it is safe to say the whole ordeal did change them. How could it not? Though we are not given further details of their life in Scripture, I do believe this experience strengthened them and their walk with God for the rest of their lives.

This, too, would become our story as God walked with Todd and I through our fiery trial. We could have chosen the path of least resistance and ended the marriage. Yes, it still would have been painfully difficult but staying proved to be hard in a much different way. In the course of time, God would use the fiery trial to ultimately burn off everything that bound us, and years later, when we finally emerged, there would be no smell of our broken marriage anywhere lingering on us. Only God can save so completely.

While I am beyond grateful for the healing God has brought into our lives, the problem with not smelling like our past is that no one knows where we've been. Meaning, as I've already mentioned, it's so easy in our social media–driven "Hey, look at this perfect snapshot of my life" era for others to write a false narrative. If you look at me today, you see a writer, a counselor, and an ordained pastor with a husband who champions her in ministry, two fantastic adult children, and the new addition of a son-in-law we love as our own child. It looks like a great life and it is, but please hear me, it is a life born out of pain, blood, sweat, and tears as I fiercely cling to my Savior, daily, seeking the healing, hope, and strength only he can bring to live faithfully in our broken world. It is a life still in process with new problems, accompanied by new lessons of God's grace and new mercies every morning.

Yes, God answered my prayers to save my marriage and family, but beyond this, far too many more prayers have gone unanswered.

Those I love have died of cancer and Alzheimer's disease. Awful tragedies have descended on those I care about who follow Jesus faithfully. We have experienced painful job loss, ministry and church hurt, and depths of pain around things our children struggled with that brought us to our knees with no one but God to look to for help. God is good, and he has redeemed parts of my story, but there are other parts where he simply gave me himself and that has proven to be enough.

I have not in any way "arrived" at a place of perfection on my faith journey. This side of glory, I will always struggle with sin and seek my Lord's forgiveness, but I am in process. As I've learned lessons of God's faithfulness along the way, he has simply beckoned me to share them with you. Today it is the lessons from my past of grace, redemption, and hope. In the future, I'm sure there will be new lessons to impart. For now, I simply want to remain obedient to share what I know.

The words from "Streams in the Desert: December 19" echo in my soul as my marching orders, reminding me to "call back" to you regarding what God has and still is teaching me...

> *If you have gone a little way ahead of me,*
> *call back—*
> *It will cheer my heart and help my feet*
> *along the stony track;*
> *And if, perhaps, Faith's light is dim,*
> *because the oil is low,*
> *Your call will guide my lagging course*
> *as wearily I go.*
>
> *Call back, and tell me*
> *that He went with you into the storm;*
> *Call back, and say He kept you*
> *when the forest's roots were torn;*
> *That, when the heavens thunder*
> *and the earthquake shook the hill,*

He bore you up and held you
where the lofty air was still.

O friend, call back, and tell me
for I cannot see your face;
They say it glows with triumph,
and your feet sprint in the race;
But there are mists between us
and my spirit eyes are dim,
And I cannot see the glory,
though I long for word of Him.

But if you'll say He heard you
when your prayer was but a cry,
And if you'll say He saw you
through the night's sin-darkened sky—
If you have gone a little way ahead,
O friend, call back—
It will cheer my heart and help my feet
along the stony track.

This book, my story, is me attempting with all my heart to "call back" to you of the faithfulness of Jesus. I have witnessed his power to heal. I have experienced his strength to hold me and support me when I had none of my own. I have received his grace and mercy for the failings of my past. And I have come to a place of daily walking with him as my friend. I may be a little farther down the road than you in my faith journey or you may be well ahead of me. Either way, may these words encourage you to keep trusting that God *is* with you on your journey.

⌘

There are many stories in Scripture that I could leave you with, but I want to take you to the one verse that brings me to tears and clenches my throat, every single time I read it. In John 4, we read that Jesus has come to a well in the heat of the day. There he meets and begins speaking to a Samaritan woman. She has made a mess of her life with five husbands in her past and is currently living with a man who was not her husband. To say her life was a wreck would be an understatement. Still, Jesus engages her in conversation and begins to tell her about "living water" and the life he could give to her if she would but ask for it. She knows enough about religion to believe he is a prophet and acknowledges that one day, the Messiah will come. This is when Jesus speaks the words that level me, "I, the one speaking to you—I am he" (John 4:26 NIV).

It leaves me undone every time I read these words. Tears are blinding me even now as I try to type them. As of yet in the biblical story, Jesus has not yet announced to anyone that he is the Messiah, and yet here, he makes the calculated decision to reveal the truth of his identity as the Messiah to a woman, but more than that, a very broken woman still living a sinful life. What in the world was he thinking? Surely, there would have been someone, more wholesome, more deserving of receiving this revelation?

Every time I read these words, my mind races back to my living room that day so long ago when I was frantically searching for Sydney. I was such a mess and yet the Lord still chose to burst into my life, whispering to my young doubting heart, "Steph, I am here and I'm real." Why? Why reveal himself to me when I was so lost and broken? Why did he keep coming for that jacked-up little girl?

In John's narrative, once Jesus reveals himself to the Samaritan woman, she immediately returns to town and tells anyone who will listen that she has met the Messiah. Her words, her intensity, her faith in how Jesus broke into her story entices them to come and see for themselves if this Jesus is really who she says, the long-awaited Messiah. Many do come, also finding themselves enamored by his words and presence; so much so that they urge Jesus to stay with them for two days, many coming to faith in him.

So why did Jesus choose the Samaritan woman? Because he knew, even before she did, that once redemption had found her, she would tell her story to the world, and in doing so, many would come to faith. Her story brought many people to Jesus, but Jesus himself captured their hearts as Scripture tells us, "They said to the woman, 'We no longer believe just because of what you said; now we have heard for ourselves, and we know that this man really is the Savior of the world'" (John 4:42 NIV).

So why did Jesus reveal himself to me? Because he knew, even before I did, that I, too, like the Samaritan woman, would one day tell our story and give him all the praise and glory for what he had done, in the hopes that others would be drawn to faith in him. Yes, God has asked for everything from me, but in return, he has given me everything I have ever needed. To him be the glory, forever and ever.

෨

Lord Jesus, my Friend, my God, my King, my Everything, my prayer to you now is for the one who is setting this book down. I pray, like the Samaritan woman, you would use my story to draw them unto yourself, and that then they would forget about me and my story and see only you. I pray you would find them, wherever they may be on their faith journey (lost, seeking, stable, or thriving), and reveal your presence in a way they can understand. Remind them that no one, no matter how broken their past may be, or how chaotic their present may seem, will be rejected by you when they come to you in faith, believing in your power to redeem. Jesus, may all who seek you, find you, and may they come to know the joy that truly comes from giving you—everything. Amen.

Epilogue

Everything Else

Listen to my heart, can't you hear it sings
telling me to give you everything.

—*Moulin Rouge* soundtrack,
"Come What May"

The *Moulin Rouge* soundtrack may seem like an odd place to find a song that so perfectly captures what life has been like with God since the day I began surrendering everything to him. Nonetheless, "Come What May" captures quite exquisitely the way I feel. Come what may, highs and lows, sorrow or joy, pain or pleasure, my Jesus is present with me in it all, and I will remain faithful to his call to continue surrendering every part of my life.

Arriving back in Missouri did not mark the end of things God would ask me to surrender. Over the next seventeen years, he would ask me to surrender my career by going back to school for ministry and counseling. He could ask for my pride as I became a forty-year-old pastoral intern. There would be the deep pain of surrendering each of my children into God's care through various choices and struggles they would each learn to navigate. Still, God kept coming, asking for more areas of surrender.

In the years to come, we would financially surpass the life we had given up before moving to Texas, eventually purchasing our dream home and all the fun toys that accompanied our lifestyle.

Only to seven years later surrender it all as Todd gave up his career to follow me into a full-time pastoral role at a church in a different state. Then COVID would hit five months into our move, hijacking much of what we thought that season of ministry would bring. My love for God's church and walking with his people would now be surrendered as we moved back to an area near St. Louis so I could counsel part-time and finally write our story.

I can honestly say, this is not what I thought my life would look like at this point and yet it is still good in ways that are surprising and beautiful. Every year, my Lord seems to come, asking for more and more, and in ways, I feel inadequate to articulate in words, he has shown me that he is worth it. Everything I have surrendered has been purposeful, and I have no regrets, for in every moment of release, God in return has given me more of himself, and I find my soul at peace.

My story is very much still in process and will be until the day I enter glory. So with much anticipation, I wonder, "What will God ask for next?"

About the Author

Stephanie Ehmke is an ordained pastor, storyteller, and licensed professional counselor with a master's degree from Covenant Theological Seminary in St. Louis, MO. She is a passionate advocate of hope and proclaims its efficacy through the power of story and scripture. Stephanie currently serves as the Location Pastor of Grace Ann Arbor West, part of the Grace Church Network in Michigan. Connect with her at www.StephanieEhmke.com or on social media @StephanieEhmke.